# America Fights the Tide

# AMERICA FIGHTS THE TIDE
## *1942*

John Devaney

**Walker and Company
New York**

This book is dedicated to U.S. Army Air Corps
flyers Bill Farrow, Dena Hallmark, and Harold
Spatz, executed by the Japanese at Shanghai on
October 15, 1942, and to the thousands of other
men and women who gave their lives in 1942
fighting for the Four Freedoms.

First published in the United States of America in 1991
by Walker Publishing Company, Inc.

Published simultaneously in Canada
by Thomas Allen & Son
Canada, Limited, Markham, Ontario

Library of Congress Cataloging-in-Publication Data
Devaney, John.
America fights the tide: 1942 / by John Devaney.
p. cm.
Includes bibliographical references and index.
Summary: Brief vignettes, photographs, and maps describe
the Second World War in 1942, from the viewpoint of
soldiers in foxholes, sailors aboard ships, pilots in fighter
planes, and soldiers landing on enemy-held beaches.
ISBN 0-8027-6998-5 (reinf.) — ISBN 0-8027-6997-7 (trade)
1. World War, 1939–1945 — Juvenile literature. 2. World
War, 1939–1945 — United States — Juvenile
literature. [1. World War, 1939–1945.] I. Title.
D755.4.D48 1991
940.54'1273 — dc20 90-29103
CIP
AC

Printed in the United States of America

2 4 6 8 10 9 7 5 3 1

# America Fights the
# Tide

# PROLOGUE

On September 1, 1939, German dictator Adolf Hitler sent his armored armies pouring into Poland, beginning World War II. England and France declared war on Germany. Hitler swiftly conquered Poland, then turned and swept over France. England's battered and bloodied army escaped to England. Hitler's armies poised to invade England and make Hitler the master of western Europe. He had signed a peace treaty with Russian dictator Josef Stalin giving the Russians what was left of Europe.

Germany had two Axis partners, Italy and Japan. Japan's military leaders convinced Emperor Hirohito that Japan should grab the land and natural riches of European-owned colonies in Southeast Asia. The English, French, and Dutch, who owned those colonies, were now too weakened by war to defend them. America's president, Franklin Delano Roosevelt, warned Japan not to grab land owned by someone else.

As 1941 began, German bombers set afire English cities. Only a few thousand young men were left to fight Hitler. They were the pilots of the Royal Air Force. They rose in their skinny Spitfires to ward off waves of Luftwaffe bombers. Most R.A.F. pilots were eighteen to twenty-two years old. Of them, the British leader, ruddy-faced Winston Churchill, told the world, "Never in the history of human warfare have so many owed so much to so few."

American volunteers joined those young British pilots. British cities burned night and day for much of the next six months. Thousands of civilians died in the flames, but the British refused to surrender. Early in 1941 Hitler decided to turn against Soviet Russia. He needed Russian oil for his tanks and planes and Russian wheat for his troops. Hitler's peace treaty with Russia had lulled Russia's dictator, Josef Stalin, into thinking that Hitler would leave him alone. Hitler told his generals to attack Russia early in May.

First, however, Hitler decided he needed millions more troops to attack a country as vast as Russia, so he twisted the arms of leaders in Bulgaria, Rumania, and Yugoslavia—the Balkan nations of southern Europe—and they agreed to send troops to join the Axis armies.

Hitler's Axis co-leader, Benito Mussolini of Italy, had attacked Greece unsuccessfully. In North Africa, Italian troops had struck at the British in Egypt—and again staggered backward, badly defeated. Hitler promised to help Mussolini conquer Greece and North Africa.

Hitler sent one of his smartest tank generals, Erwin Rommel, to North Africa to form an Afrika Korps, and the Germans massed troops in Bulgaria and Rumania to attack Greece.

Then Hitler got a nasty surprise. The Yugoslavian people rose up and refused to join the Axis. That made Hitler pause. If he attacked Greece, Yugoslavian troops could pounce on his tanks from their mountaintops. Hitler had to delay the attack on Russia, which he called Operation Barbarossa, while he punished the Yugoslavs for refusing to join the Axis.

Savage air attacks killed thousands of men, women, and children in Belgrade, the Yugoslav capital. Yugoslavia fell. Within a month, so did Greece. And on June 22, a month later than he had planned, Hitler's Panzer divisions drove into Russia and routed the surprised Russians. By late summer German tanks had smashed within 200 miles of Moscow. But Hitler wanted oil and wheat right away, so he ordered his generals to turn away from Moscow and plunge south to capture the Ukraine, where there were vast amounts of oil and wheat. The Germans captured the Ukraine within a month, and Hitler's tanks turned north to drive once more toward Moscow. But his soldiers in their summer uniforms felt the first stinging blasts of the icy Russian winter.

In North Africa, meanwhile, Rommel's new Afrika Korps blasted the British out of Libya and crashed into Egypt. If Rommel could capture Egypt, the Suez Canal would be his. India and Australia were sending lifesaving food to England through that canal. Rommel stood within a few hundred miles of cutting off that lifeline—and only the shattered, dazed British army blocked his way.

Rommel could not cross Egypt's desert without water for his troops and tanks. He could get that water only at the Libyan port of Tobruk, where British, Australian, and New Zealand troops had dug in. Rommel threw wave after wave of tanks and infantry at Tobruk's sun-scorched defenders. But the "Rats of Tobruk" held the city and the water.

In Japan military men and politicians had convinced Emperor Hirohito that Japan might have to go to war to get the land and raw materials of Southeast Asia. They had drawn up a war plan: they would invade French Indochina (today's Vietnam), British Malaya, and the Dutch East Indies. The defeated French and Dutch had no army or navy to defend their colonies. But the British had an army in Malaya. Two British battleships were roaming the Indian Ocean to guard England's naval base of Singapore at the tip of Malaya.

Japan's leaders knew that a thrust south at Malaya and the Philippines meant war with Great Britain and America. To win that war, Japan decided on a two-fisted attack. One task force of warships, aircraft carriers, and troop ships would attack Southeast Asia. Another task force of aircraft carriers would sneak silently across the Pacific and send its planes to bomb the American fleet anchored at Pearl Harbor. If America's Pacific Fleet were destroyed, America would need years to rebuild another one. By then Japan would be entrenched in Southeast Asia.

Roosevelt did not want war with Japan. He wanted to join Churchill in defeating Hitler. He knew America was not ready to fight both in Europe and in Asia. He was trying to build up America's military muscle and was drafting millions of men into the army. He talked Congress into spending billions of dollars to build tanks, planes, and warships. Most Americans agreed that their country should be strong enough to defend itself against an attack by Hitler or Japan, but few wanted to go to war to help Britain.

Roosevelt used his popularity—he was the first president elected to three terms—to get the Lend-Lease law passed by Congress. That law allowed him to send warships, planes, guns, tanks, oil, and food to England. Hitler tried to cut off that supply. His submarines torpedoed ships crossing the Atlantic to England. One German U-boat sank an American destroyer convoying ships. By the fall of 1941, Roosevelt knew America was edging toward war with Hitler.

Then came a climactic December. In Russia, Hitler's armies battled through snowstorms toward Moscow. The Russians threw millions of fresh Siberian troops into a surprise counter-attack. The weary, frostbitten Germans staggered backward, then ran for their lives. Hitler fired his top generals and took over as commander in chief. But at year's end, the German armies had suffered their worst defeat.

In North Africa Rommel's Afrika Korps lost most of its tanks as England's Eighth Army pushed him back from Tobruk. Now it was Rommel's turn to run. By Christmas the Eighth Army had swept the Afrika Korps out of Egypt and back into the Italian colony of Libya where Rommel had started.

Early in December Japan's envoys in Washington offered a last-minute deal to avert war. If Roosevelt stopped sending aid to Chiang Kai-shek in China, they said, Japan would not invade Southeast Asia. Roosevelt said no. First, he did not trust the Japanese, and second, he did not want to hand over China to Japan. Japan's leader, Prime Minister Hideki Tojo, then ordered his generals and admirals to go to war and to begin the war with a surprise attack on Pearl Harbor.

At dawn on December 7, almost 400 Japanese bombers took off from six aircraft carriers and struck at sleeping American sailors on their ships at Pearl Harbor. Some two hours later more than a thousand Americans were dead, and a half-dozen American warships were ablaze. An angry Roosevelt declared war on Japan. Hitler joined his Axis ally by declaring war on America.

The Japanese plunged south to attack the Philippines and Malaya. By Christmas they had captured Manila and thrust within a few miles of Singapore. With Manila their "front door" and Singapore their "back door," the Japanese could lock up the riches of Southeast Asia.

As 1941 ended, America's Philippine army, commanded by General Douglas MacArthur, retreated into the jungle peninsula of Bataan. As long as MacArthur held Bataan and the guns of its island fortress, Corregidor, the Japanese could not use Manila as their "front door" to Southeast Asia.

Just before Christmas, Churchill arrived in Washington. He and Roosevelt agreed that Hitler should be beaten first and then the two Allies would defeat Japan. By New Year's Eve more than twenty other nations had joined America and England in the war against the Axis. Sitting up in his wheelchair until almost 3:00 A.M. on New Year's Day, 1942, Roosevelt coined a name for the Allies: the United Nations.

As 1942 began, the German tide had been stopped in Russia and North Africa, but the tide was gathering strength to rush back toward Moscow and Cairo. In the Pacific the Japanese tide was sweeping west toward India and east toward the Pacific coast of America. Japanese submarines scuttled along the shore off Los

Angeles and San Francisco. And only fifty miles off the East Coast, German submarine commanders peered through their periscopes at the twinkling lights of Manhattan, Washington, Charleston, and Miami. Americans looked up at the skies and asked one another, "When will the bombers that burned London and Pearl Harbor be roaring over us?"

# Chapter One

**JAN. 1:** *The White House, the President's study*

A cold, drenching rain had fallen all afternoon and evening. Cigar clenched in his teeth, the plump, apple-cheeked Winston Churchill sat across the room from President Roosevelt. Sitting nearby were the slim, spectacled T. V. Soong, representing China, and the burly Soviet ambassador, Maxim Litvinoff. Since early afternoon the four had made changes in a document now neatly typed and perched on Roosevelt's desk. Picking up a fountain pen, Roosevelt scribbled at the top of the first page, "Declaration by United Nations, Done at Washington January 1, 1942. The United States of America, by Franklin D. Roosevelt."

An aide handed the document to Churchill, who wrote, "The United Kingdom of Great Britain and Northern Ireland, by Winston Churchill."

Litvinoff signed for Russia, Soong for China. A State Department official said twenty-two other nations would sign the next day: Australia, Belgium, Canada, Costa Rica,

Cuba, Czechoslovakia, the Dominican Republic, El Salvador, Greece, Guatemala, Haiti, Honduras, India, Luxembourg, the Netherlands, New Zealand, Nicaragua, Norway, Panama, Poland, South Africa, and Yugoslavia.

Each of the twenty-six United Nations pledged its full might, "military or economic," against the Axis powers "for complete victory" to "preserve human rights and justice."

Churchill puffed contentedly on his cigar. A year ago he had stood alone against the Axis. "Now," he murmured to an aide, "we have four-fifths of the world with us."

### JAN. 2: *Bataan, a crossroads*

Colonel Ernie Miller couldn't sleep, even though he was exhausted after days of combat. His 194th Tank Battalion had fought off Japanese tanks at Calumpit Bridge while MacArthur's army marched wearily in retreat over the bridge into the jungles of Bataan. The Bataan peninsula stuck like a bony finger toward Manila Bay and the rocky island fortress of Corregidor. Colonel Miller worried about what he had seen at Calumpit—empty trucks rolling across the bridge. MacArthur's last-minute decision to retreat into Bataan had surprised his supply officers. They had left behind tons of food that could have fed Bataan's defenders for a year. Now there might not be enough food even for a month.

"I have a hunch we're going to get hit," a

captain said to Miller, glancing at his watch. It was almost 2:00 A.M. as a bright moon spilled yellow light over rice paddies and thick jungle.

A rifle shot blasted the silence. Miller and the captain scrambled onto their tanks. They heard howls that reminded Miller of Apache yells he'd heard in Western movies. One shriek pierced the howling: "We are the peepul who are not afraid to die by boolets!"

Crouched behind his machine gun, Miller saw the waves of brown uniforms surging across the moonlit paddy. The Japanese soldiers, an American tanker said later, "looked like badly wrapped brown paper packages." Their legs were short, their pants baggy, their blouses loose. "They didn't charge," one American said. "They crouched forward just a little bit, lifting their knees in a sort of goose-step. They came at you in pairs, one directly behind the other."

American tanks spit bullets from heavy automatic machine guns. The wall of fire stopped the wave for a minute, but then it surged forward again. The Japanese were firing light .25-caliber one-shot rifles. They fired, bent down to reload, then stood to fire again.

A Japanese bullet hit a gasoline container. Balls of flame shot upward, turning the moonlight into bright day. Now, for the first time, the Japanese could see the American tanks. The flames silhouetted the tanks against the blackness of the jungle. Japanese mortars dropped shells around the tanks, the deafening blasts shaking the tanks. Hunks of iron shrapnel whizzed by soldiers crouched around the tanks.

Lieutenant Dan Petree leaped off his tank to stomp out one blaze. Kneeling high in the limbs of a tree, a Japanese sniper watched Petree come between the cross hairs of his sight. He fired and Petree dropped, a bullet in his back.

*He shot Petree in the back!* Anger boiled up inside Colonel Miller. Modern soldiers, he believed, fought fairly, not like savages shooting enemies in the back. He wheeled around his machine gun and sprayed the tree. Three brown-bloused bodies tumbled to earth.

The Japanese fired white flares to show succeeding waves how far they had pierced the American line. In the eerie white light Miller could see stacks of bodies piled up in the rice paddy, legs and arms splayed at crazy angles like rag dolls.

Darkness again dropped like a black cloak over the paddies as the chattering guns stuttered into silence. The shrieks of the wounded Japanese—Miller guessed at least a hundred—faded as comrades pulled them into the jungle.

Colonel Miller began to count his dead and wounded, about a dozen. He looked into the hungry, bearded, sweaty faces of his tankers. He knew that no one was looking forward to another suicide attack by those little jungle fighters "who are not afraid to die by boolets!"

**JAN. 3:** *Washington, the War Department*

Wearing his new one star proudly, Brigadier General Dwight David Eisenhower—his pals called him "Ike"—was getting his first orders from his boss, four-star General George Marshall, the Army chief of staff. A few months earlier, Marshall had admired the wizardry of Colonel Eisenhower as Ike moved troops like a chess master during maneuvers in Louisiana. Marshall promoted Ike and made him chief of war planning. Now Marshall asked Ike how America could get help to MacArthur on Bataan.

Ike said the Navy was not willing to risk its Pacific Fleet to convoy troops and cargo ships more than 3,000 miles from Hawaii to the Philippines. He knew, however, that if MacArthur's trapped 100,000-man army had to surrender, American hearts—sickened by Pearl Harbor—would sink even lower. He said he would try to send supplies to MacArthur's troops by submarine. Marshall told Ike, "Do your best to save them."

**JAN. 4:** *Seattle, Washington, Navy Recruiting Center*

Fifty-one-year-old Walter Bromley tried to enlist. A sailor told him he was six years too old. A few hours later, Bromley was sworn into the Navy as a seaman third class. The age limit was waived for Bromley after he explained that his two sons had died at Pearl Harbor.

**JAN. 4:** *Corregidor, MacArthur's office in the underground Malinta Tunnel*

G eneral MacArthur scanned the cable from Washington, then handed it to General Dick Sutherland, his chief of staff. Nearby sat Jean MacArthur, who cradled the MacArthurs' three-year-old son, Arthur, in her lap. "Sir Boss," as she lovingly called her husband, told her that the cable was from Marshall and Roosevelt. "It says," MacArthur said, "that help is on the way." But the message did not say how much help and when it would arrive.

MacArthur knew the spirits of his tired and hungry soldiers on Bataan needed a lift. He sent this message to them: "Help is on the way from the United States. Thousands of troops and hundreds of planes are being dispatched. The exact time of arrival of reinforcement is unknown. . . . It is imperative that our troops hold until these reinforcement arrives. No further retreat is possible . . ."

Soldiers shinnied up trees on Bataan, scrambling to the tops to scan the sea. Each soldier wanted to be the first to spot the masts of the ships coming over the horizon to rescue them.

Each night they came down disappointed— and hungry. MacArthur ordered his troops on half rations. The cans of food on Bataan and Corregidor were dwindling fast. Eight GIs, as they called themselves (GI meant Government Issue), had to live on one can of salmon a day.

But rumors still sped from one foxhole to

the next: "Ten thousand troops have landed and started toward Manila." "A thousand bombers are lined up in Australia and will start to bomb the Japanese on Bataan tomorrow or the next day." "I heard that a huge convoy of troop ships and battleships are within a day of here."

**JAN. 6:** *Washington, the White House, the Oval Office*
The slim, bony-faced visitor fiddled nervously with his steel-rimmed glasses. Missouri Senator Harry Truman had always been a loyal, hardworking Democrat. Now he worried that the Boss, as he called Roosevelt, had called him in for a scolding.

Truman headed a Senate committee that had toured America's war factories. They had checked on the guns, tanks, and planes rolling out of the factories. Truman saw guns that blew up, tanks that fell apart, planes that crashed. His committee publicly accused company owners and labor unions of "greed, gross inefficiency, graft, corruption and profiteering horrors."

Republicans clapped their hands with glee as horrified Americans read the Truman report. This Democratic president, Republicans said, was making a mess of the war effort. Republicans were boosting General MacArthur, "a real war leader," as their candidate for president in 1944.

Truman knew his report had embarrassed the Boss. He tried to explain to his party's leader why he had felt it a duty to make the report public. At one factory making bombers, Truman said, he asked the company's owner why so many of his bombers crashed. The crashes had killed a dozen Air Corps pilots.

"The wing spread is too short," the owner said.

"Make the wings wider," Truman said.

"Can't. I won't make as much money on the planes if I make the wings wider."

"What?" Truman screeched. "Are you willing to kill American boys just to make a profit?"

Truman forced the company to widen the wings. But sloppy workers and greedy business leaders, he told the President, were costing the lives of soldiers and sailors. "I'm asking $100,000 more to continue investigating," Truman said with a glance at the Boss, adding, "but I'll call it off if you say the word."

"No, Harry," the President said. "I want you to continue." As the square-shouldered Truman marched out of the room, Roosevelt knew he had to find a strongman to run the war factories so that America's soldiers, sailors, and airmen got weapons to kill the enemy and not themselves.

**JAN. 8:** *New York City*

Public school students returned after Christmas holidays to assemblies where principals spoke to them about what to do in case of

Heavyweight boxing champion Joe Louis is inducted into the army early in 1942 in New York. Usually shy and poker-faced, he surprised friends with the impromptu statement that America would win the war because "God is on our side." The champion is wearing his first "dog tag," a numbered disc worn around the neck by servicemen to identify them in case of sudden death. *(Photo from the author's collection)*

an air raid. "It is safer," the kids were told, "to stay inside the building rather than attempt to return home." Washington's Office of Civil Defense was issuing the same warning to all schools on the East Coast.

## JAN. 10: *Geneva, Switzerland*

A writer for the *Journal de Geneve,* a newspaper in neutral Switzerland, visited cities across Nazi-occupied Europe. He saw starving people, farmlands devastated, and mobs of children digging for food scraps in garbage pails outside army camps.

"In Athens," the reporter wrote, "a loaf of bread costs $15. I was told that 2,000 died of starvation in one day." Relatives did not report deaths, secretly burying the corpses. They kept the corpse's food-ration card to get extra rations. Thousands of emaciated Greeks floated in small boats toward Turkey, begging for life.

## JAN. 13: *Washington, the White House*

Donald M. Nelson, a six-foot-two-inch, 195-pound "efficiency executive" for a department store, puffed on his pipe as Roosevelt introduced him to reporters. "This is the head of the new War Production Board," Roosevelt said. Nelson would be the "dictator" to make sure that America's war factories turned out the best planes, tanks, guns, and warships the world had ever seen.

"By 1943 we'll be launching two ships a day," Nelson told reporters. "We'll be rolling out a plane every two minutes, a tank every seven minutes."

Americans, he said, would not be able to buy a new car, a new refrigerator, even a new toaster, radio, or phonograph "for the duration." (The new phrase meant "until the war is over.")

**JAN. 12:** *Washington, the White House, the Cabinet Room*

B ritish and American generals and admirals were arguing loudly. As Roosevelt and Churchill listened, the military and naval strategists were giving their theories on the best way to defeat Hitler.

General Marshall presented the American plan—a straight-ahead punch thrown from England and aimed at Hitler's chin and heart. British and American troops would cross the English Channel and invade France and ram straight ahead to Berlin.

No, growled Churchill. He and the British people had no heart for a frontal assault. In World War I German guns had blown away millions of British young men as they charged across French battlefields. A generation of manhood had been lost.

Why not stab "the soft underbelly" of Hitler's empire? Churchill argued. His strategy: Land in North Africa and capture the entire Mediterranean shore of Africa. From those beaches an Allied army could hop across the Mediterranean to knife into southern Europe—Hitler's "soft underbelly."

Roosevelt yearned for "a face-to-face battle" with the Axis as soon as possible. The 1942 elections to Congress would be held in the fall. He wanted military victories by then so American voters would elect Democrats to Congress. Democrats would vote into law Roosevelt's ideas on fighting the war.

Roosevelt and Churchill knew that Uncle Joe, as Roosevelt called Stalin, was demanding a "second front"—an invasion that would force Hitler to turn and stop hitting the Russians so hard.

Stalin wanted an invasion of France. Churchill was arguing that invading France should come later, when the Americans and English would have built up larger forces.

Roosevelt offered a compromise: an invasion of North Africa in 1942, an invasion of France in 1943.

The meeting ended with Churchill agreeing to an invasion of North Africa later in 1942. Generals Marshall and Eisenhower told each other they would go on planning for an invasion of France in the fall of 1942. When Churchill went back to England, Marshall told

Ike, he would try to convince Roosevelt that the smash at the heart of Germany should take place as soon as possible.

Ike agreed. "We will never forgive ourselves," he told Marshall, "if we lose the eight-million-man Russian army . . . because we didn't come to their aid in 1942 with an invasion of France."

**JAN. 14:** *Washington, the White House*

As commander in chief, President Roosevelt issued a proclamation ordering all "enemy aliens"—citizens of Japan, Germany, and Italy living in the United States—to register immediately with officials in their cities or towns. Any enemy alien who did not register within a week would be arrested.

**JAN. 14:** *Washington, the Department of Justice*

U.S. Attorney General Francis Biddle told newspaper reporters, radio microphones, and newsreel cameras that twenty-seven zones in the United States must be swept clear of enemy aliens by February 15. These included cities, towns, villages, and farms near army camps, naval bases, ship-

Signs posted in the window of a shop in Los Angeles owned by Japanese-Americans early in 1942. Despite their protests that they were "100 percent American citizens," this shop and others owned by Japanese-Americans had to be given up, their owners transferred to inland camps for the duration. *(Photo courtesy of The Library of Congress)*

yards, and war factories. Many of the zones were in California's coastal cities.

**JAN. 15:** *The Atlantic, forty miles off Long Island*

The *Norness* skipper, Harold Hansen, could see the lights of Long Island, 100 miles from Manhattan, as the first torpedo slammed into the oil tanker. A second torpedo hit midships, setting off two explosions. Hansen saw the bodies of two of his crew twirling high in the air, outlined against the flames lighting up the midnight sky.

A minute later he was thrashing in the icy cold water, trying to hold on to a raft with numbed fingers. He saw two figures running across the tanker's deck as flames licked at their heels. Both men vanished within the cherry-red flames.

A third torpedo set off an ear-shattering explosion. Hansen watched his tanker break in half and vanish amid churning water. One hundred yards away, the German U-boat rose, its prow swinging to face the rafts. Machine-gun bullets spattered in the water around the rafts, two of them whizzing by Hansen's shoulders.

Then came darkness and quiet. Hansen heard cries. Of the forty crewmen of the *Norness,* thirty-eight had been thrown into the water and were still alive. An hour later, a Coast Guard cutter picked up the freezing survivors and took them to New York.

"I thought we were just as safe before the

torpedo hit," Hansen said, "as we would have been in New York harbor."

### JAN. 15: *Sacramento, California*

California's Attorney General Earl Warren said he was studying how and when to clear enemy aliens from areas near war camps and war factories.

"There are 93,000 Japanese in California who are both American and Japanese citizens," the balding, heavyset Warren said. "It is impossible to distinguish between enemy aliens genuinely loyal to the United States and those who may be saboteurs and spies."

### JAN. 16: *British Malaya, thirty miles north of Singapore*

Two British soldiers, one from London, the other from Edinburgh, crouched in a roadside ditch. They were part of a machine gun squad guarding the rear of General Sir Arthur Percival's army as it retreated down the Malayan peninsula toward the island fortress of Singapore.

"Blimey," said the London soldier. "Those Japanese won't fight in the open. They aren't soldiers. They're more like bloody monkeys."

"Aye," said the soldier from Edinburgh. "You got to be like Tarzan to catch them."

The road behind them ran straight into the jungle. "Seems clear," said the London soldier, standing to pick up the barrel of the machine gun.

The first mortar shell, lobbed out of that seemingly empty wall of green, blew within thirty feet of the London soldier, knocking him into the ditch. The Edinburgh soldier raced to a nearby house. He threw open the door and fell, facedown, on the dirt floor. He clasped his hands over his helmet as mortar blasts shook the wooden house. Later, in a hospital, he told a surgeon, "The next thing I remember is seeing my own left arm landing on the other side of the room."

JAN. 16: *Hollywood, California*

Passersby smiled as the grocery store owner was posting this sign on his window:

"We are legal Japanese. Our 2 Sons Are in the U.S. Army."

JAN. 19: *New York City, Madison Square Garden*

No boxer had ever done it before, risking a million-dollar world title for charity. Heavyweight champion Joe Louis was taking on 230-pound Buddy Baer for the world title—and donating his $100,000-plus purse to the Navy Relief Fund. The money would go to needy families of sailors.

The Navy held a luncheon at the arena on the early afternoon of the fight. An officer asked the champion to come up to the ring and speak to the 2,000 guests.

The Brown Bomber, as newspapers called him, walked to the ring, stepped through the ropes, and held a microphone. Poker-faced and soft-spoken, he seldom said more than a few words before or after a fight. He said he would soon join the Army and help win the war. "And we will win," he said, "because we are on God's side."

That night he knocked out Baer in the first round. The next morning he held up his right hand and was sworn in as a private in the United States Army.

**JAN. 18–20:** *Near Bryanmskky, Russia*

Private soldier Gerhardt Ballach served as a chaffeur to officers at this sector's general headquarters. Headquarters was fifty miles behind the front lines, where German troops had stopped retreating at Hitler's orders. They had dug in to stop fierce attacks by the Siberian troops who had routed Hitler's armies within ten miles of Moscow.

The Germans faced bullets in front of them, behind them, and at their flanks. Men and women and teenage guerrilla fighters—called Partisans—had joined what Stalin trumpeted as the Great Patriotic War. The Partisans came out at night to ambush and kill Germans, sometimes with small hunting rifles, sometimes with kitchen knives, sometimes with bare hands.

Ballach was keeping a diary. "In the evening we left in two columns to chase the elusive guerrillas. Hermann's detachment was attacked by them and private first class Gernitz was killed by a shot in the head. This came as a very profound shock to us. . . . Monday, we strung up a Russian. He was a guerrilla fighter. . . . At 5:30, a mine exploded resulting in a train wreck. At 9 five hostages were hanged, two males and three females, including two 14-year-old girls."

**JAN. 20:** *Wannsee, Germany, a Berlin suburb*

Fifteen SS officers in charge of Hitler's secret police in Germany and all of Nazi-occupied Europe had been summoned to this meeting by Reinhard Heydrich, the assistant SS chief, who had executed so many Jews and Poles in Warsaw that Nazi resistance fighters called him the Hangman.

Heydrich and his superior, Heinrich Himmler, had received secret orders from Hitler, who reminded his SS chiefs what he had said in a 1939 speech: If war comes, "the result will be . . . the annihilation of the Jewish race throughout Europe."

"In the course of this Final Solution of the European Jewish problem," Heydrich told the fifteen SS officials, "approximately eleven million Jews are involved," including 131,800 in Germany (of 250,000 in 1939), eight million in Russia, two million in Poland, and a quarter of a million in "soon to be conquered England."

The Hangman explained to the SS chiefs the step-by-step procedure for the Final Solution.

The first WAACs, attending the Women's Auxiliary Army Corps' Officers Candidate School at Fort Des Moines, Iowa, obey the order to "dress left." In close-order drills like this, a soldier establishes with the right or left arm a distance of forty inches from the soldier on the right or left. The WAACs later become the WACs, the Women's Army Corps. *(Photo courtesy of the National Archives)*

Jews would be transported to Poland and Russia, organized into all-men and all-women labor gangs, and worked so hard that most would die. To speed up the Final Solution, concentration camps—places like Auschwitz and Treblinka, which had been used to gas to death small numbers of Jews, gypsies, and other "undesirables"—would now be turned into "Vernichtungslager"—mass extermination camps.

**JAN. 26:** *Washington, Capitol Hill*

Reporters gathered in the office of Massachusetts Congresswoman Edith Nourse Rogers. The tall, graying Rogers outlined her bill, now before Congress, that would establish the Women's Auxiliary Army Corps (WAAC).

The WAACs, all volunteers, would go through basic training, wear uniforms, skirts or slacks, and get the same pay as men in the Army. They would be subject to military discipline under women officers but would not be sent into combat.

"Would they go overseas into combat areas?" a reporter asked.

"Yes," Rogers said. "They will work as clerks, drivers, typists, cooks and at other jobs in rear-areas only."

The age limit, she added, was forty-five, and that had set off protests. "I am 58," one Shrewsbury, Mass., woman wrote to Rogers, "and I can drive and work as good, if not better, than some men."

Rogers read a letter from a seventeen-year-old high school girl in Fountain City, Tennessee, who told the Congresswoman why she would volunteer to be a WAAC.

"I read about the Marines who fought to defend Wake Island. They made me so proud and I only wish I could have been there with them."

**JAN. 26:** *Belfast, Northern Ireland*
The Royal Ulster Rifles Marching Band stood on the dock and played "The Star Spangled Banner." Major General Russell Hartle came down the gangplank. He was followed by Private First Class Millburn Henke, a twenty-two-year-old Yank (as the British called GIs) from Minnesota. They were the first troops to land in Europe since the end of World

War I. They were followed, as other troop ships docked, by 30,000 Yanks. The troops marched to their training camps with their bands playing George M. Cohan's World War I song, "Over There" ("The Yanks are coming . . . Over there.")

**JAN. 31:** *Near Moulmein, Burma*

E xcerpt from a diary found two months later on a Japanese officer: "4 A.M. With the battalion headquarters and regimental headquarters of 112th Infantry regiment. We struck the north edge of the Moulmein airdrome and seized the landing ground. We waited for dawn and at first light the enemy machine guns swept us with fire above our heads and made a terrific din. The battery commander received a burst of bullets in the stomach and was in critical condition. For this, a prisoner of war was killed. First, Hosogway bayoneted him, then he struck him in the belly. The prisoner did not die at once, but of course it is not permitted to waste bullets when killing prisoners of war. Straightaway, we carried on the advance to Moulmein."

**JAN. 31:** *San Francisco, California*

C ivil defense chief Charles Dullea told the city that "we are in a combat zone. The danger is grave and it's imminent. No enemy aliens will be allowed to hold civil defense jobs. The chief danger is sabotage from within by enemy aliens."

## Chapter Two

**FEB. 2:** *Msus, Libya*

Field Marshal Erwin Rommel stood on a cliff overlooking the bare, sun-scorched desert plain. A grin spread slowly on his face as his Afrika Korps' bigger M-22 tanks blew away the smaller Tiger tanks of the British Eighth Army. As the M-22 tanks poured cannon and machine fire, British tanks crawled back toward the Egyptian border, leaving behind a trail of blackened steel carcasses.

"If we can keep pushing back those Tigers," Rommel told a staff officer, "we'll cross the Plains of Msus to Tobruk." Trobruk held the fresh water that Rommel needed to cross the Sahara desert and capture Cairo and the Suez Canal. The canal was Britain's lifeline to its breadbasket in India.

A staff officer ran up to Rommel and stammered, "General, we need more fuel for our tanks!"

"Well, go and get it from the British!" Rommel snapped. Then he grinned. He had won this battle. Hundreds of new and bigger tanks—just arrived in North Africa from Germany—were roaring across the desert to help him achieve the success that had eluded him in 1941. This time, he vowed, Tobruk would fall—and so would Cairo, the biggest prize of all, 500 hot, blinding desert miles away.

**FEB. 2:** *Los Angeles, California*

FBI agents carried what they called "Presidential arrest warrants" as they rounded up more than 200 Japanese fishermen who were not American citizens. Wives and children watched as the men were led away to detention camps. "These raids may be the best way of solving the problem of suspected fifth columnist saboteurs and spies on our coast," State Attorney General Earl Warren told reporters. "But we may also have to consider an exodus of all aliens to camps in the United States interior where they can do no harm."

**FEB. 5:** *Bataan*

The Forty-Fifth Infantry Regiment's Major Dudley Stricker welcomed Air Corps Captain Allison Ind, a bomber pilot, to his command post. Ind's B-17 had been destroyed in the December 7 air raid on Clark Field. His gunners had been sent to the infantry to fight as riflemen. Ind had come to visit them.

"They're at the front, captain," Stricker said, "and the front isn't that far away."

Four GIs led Captain Ind down a narrow, winding trail into the jungle. A sergeant pointed to a pile of empty tin cans. "Salmon," he said. "That's what we live on."

"Didja bring that sirloin steak I ordered?" a voice called out.

Ind grinned, recognizing one of his gunners behind the bearded, gaunt face. The gunner was spread out on the mossy ground behind a log. His Springfield-model rifle, a World War I relic, pointed into the dark jungle.

Something whizzing by Ind's ear sounded like a buzzing mosquito. "Keep your head down," growled a machine gunner. "Those are Jap .25 slugs going by your ears."

Suddenly the jungle seemed to explode into a fury of sound. Ind heard, as he said later, "the short flat-sided snap of the Japanese .25s, the staccato cracks of the .30 Springfields mingled with machine guns and semiautomatics and tommies [Thompson submachine guns]. Then there was the strident viciousness of the .50s machine guns blasting frenziedly." Shells exploded with the thumping roar of tom-tom drums.

The ear-ringing clatter suddenly ceased. The jungle, Ind said to himself, "is as quiet as a flower-filled meadow on a Sunday afternoon."

Ind and his escorts crept cautiously on hands and knees down the trail that twisted between huge, gnarled tree trunks. They glanced upward, watchful for snipers. They heard feet pounding. Two stretcher bearers hurried down the trail. On the stretcher Ind saw the chalk-white face of a GI. He was one of his escorts. He had been caught out in a clearing during that last burst of firing.

Ind crept to the last American outpost. Two red-eyed GIs stretched out in shallow holes. They were surrounded by empty tin cans and shell casings. One GI gripped a rifle, the other a field phone. The phone line snaked 100 yards back through the jungle to the command post.

Ind winced as the acrid smell of gunpowder bit his nostrils. His stomach heaved as he smelled something else. A breeze was blowing in from the jungle, a stench so powerful that Ind thought he would retch.

The GI with the rifle smiled at the sick look on Ind's face. "Corpses," he said. "The place out there is full of 'em. And they're plenty ripe. But if you try to go out and bury the dead ones, the live ones still up in the trees will plug you. So you just let them cook like that."

Ind stuck his head carefully around a tree and saw stacks of Japanese bodies. Swarms of huge flies droned above the bodies. "They were buzzing messengers of filth," Ind wrote that night in his diary, "carrying the germs of deadly disease from the putrefying corpses that no one dared bury."

**FEB. 12:** *New York City, Bronx High School of Science*

Sophomore Bill McWeeney read the war-bond poster appearing in newspapers and magazines, schools, department stores, and movie theaters. It showed an American Revolutionary War soldier gripping a rifle. The poster's title read: "For Defense, Buy U.S. Saving Bonds and Stamps," followed by these words: "It will cost money to defeat Germany, Japan and Italy. Our government calls on you to help now. Buy defense bonds or stamps today. Buy them every day if you can."

McWeeney was on his way to an office in the school with a dollar of lunch money he had saved for a week. He bought ten ten-cent war-bond stamps and pasted them in a savings book. When he had $18.50 in stamps, he would turn in the book for a war bond. His $18.50 went to the government to help pay for the war, which was costing the U.S. Treasury more than

Farmers line up in the post office of a small town in Minnesota to buy U.S. war bonds and stamps. The bonds and stamps, loans by the people of the United States to their government during the war, were sold in schools, stores, and banks. Towns and schools—even classes in schools—competed against one another to see who could sell the most war bonds. *(Photo courtesy of The Library of Congress)*

a million dollars an hour. The Treasury promised to pay back McWeeney's loan of $18.50 with $25.00 five years from now. Of course, as war-bond buyers told one another, there was no guarantee there would be a United States Treasury to pay off that loan in faraway 1947.

**FEB. 14:** *Singapore Airport*

Fifteen-year-old Tommy Arns crouched behind sandbags that lined the runway. Arns was a "boy sailor," a cabin boy on the cruiser *Repulse* that had been sunk a few weeks earlier in the Indian Ocean. He and 400 other British boy sailors had been handed rifles and told to defend the airport. Tommy crouched behind sandbags as mortar shells crashed among the sailors. Through the smoke and evening mist, Tommy saw the ragged line of Japanese soldiers advancing across the white concrete of the runway.

"They're carrying bayonets," a sailor said to Tommy.

"A strafing Hurricane or Spitfire would give us a chance," a sailor said. "One dive bombing would give us the chance to go after them with our bayonets." But when Tommy looked up, he saw only Japanese Zeros buzzing across the sky.

The mortar shell blew bits of sandbag, bone, flesh, and blood across the concrete. Coming through the smoke and the shrieks of dying sailors, the Japanese bayoneted the wounded, including Tommy. Only a half-dozen of the boy sailors were led away, bleeding and dazed, as prisoners.

**FEB. 15:** *Singapore, a factory building*

General Sir Arthur Percival entered the room and faced General Tomoyuki Yamashita, the Tiger of Malaya. Yamashita's jungle army had swept down the Malayan peninsula on foot and bike in nine weeks while smashing a British army double its size. "I want to hear whether you want to surrender or not," Yamashita snapped. "If you want to surrender, I insist on it being unconditional."

PERCIVAL: "Will you give me until tomorrow morning?"

YAMASHITA: "If that is to be the case, the Japanese forces will have to resume the attack until then. Will you say yes or no?"

*Silence from Percival.*

YAMASHITA: "I want to have a definite answer and I insist on unconditional surrender. What do you say?"

PERCIVAL: "Yes."

He had said yes to the surrender of his 60,000-man army and England's biggest naval and air base—the worst defeat in Great Britain's history.

**FEB. 16:** *Corregidor*

The air raid sirens wailed. For almost a week, Japanese bombers had roared over the island fortress. Underground tunnels had been carved through the Rock, as Corregidor was called. The tunnels were filled with cans of food, gasoline, ammunition, and hospital beds for the wounded. In a rock-walled room off Malinta Tunnel, General MacArthur, his wife, Jean, and their three-year-old son, Arthur, heard the sirens. MacArthur hurried Jean and the toddling Arthur toward an air-raid shelter.

A bomb burst a hundred yards away. Jean and Arthur were knocked to the ground by the concussion. The General helped them to their feet and hurried them into the concrete shelter. Then he turned and walked toward soldiers who were feeding shells into rows of anti-aircraft guns. He stood among the ack-ack gunners, staring upward at the low-flying bombers. With an ear-shattering roar, a bomb blew a huge, smoking crater in the rocky ground. Smoke and throat-choking dust ringed MacArthur and the gunners. MacArthur saw a roof fly off a nearby building.

Sergeant Domingo Adversario rushed to the General. He held a steel helmet so that it shielded the face of MacArthur, who was wearing only his jaunty gold-braided cap. A sharp-edged hunk of shrapnel, hurled by an exploding bomb, tore into Adversario's hand. Mac-Arthur stared upward at the enemy, seeming not to notice the bloody wound.

For three hours he stood under the falling

bombs, as he did during all the daily air raids. "It was simply my duty," he later said. "The gunners . . . liked to see me with them." But standing under bombs can be scary even for a general, and Sergeant Adversario later said that during those bombings he felt the General's knees shaking.

MacArthur had crossed over to the Bataan peninsula one afternoon to see his troops in their jungle foxholes. He knew now that no help would be coming from America. But he wanted his troops to believe that help could come any day—so they would keep on fighting. They still climbed trees each evening to try to spot the masts of their rescuers. MacArthur could not bring himself to look into the eyes of those hungry, grimy fighting men and tell them that no help was coming. That first visit to Bataan was his last.

**FEB. 16:** *Bataan*

The soldiers around the campfire roared laughter as they began the song again to the tune of "The Battle Hymn of the Republic": "Dugout Doug lies ashakin' on the Rock, glory, glory . . ." To millions back home, who read about "Douglas MacArthur's Army on Bataan," he was the Hero of Bataan. To his soldiers on Bataan, who never saw him on Bataan—or under those bombardments on Corregidor—he was Dugout Doug.

**FEB. 17:** *Corregidor, Malinta Tunnel*

"My real enemy is behind me, in Washington," MacArthur was angrily telling his chief of staff, General Dick Sutherland. He thought he had been deserted. He blamed the Navy for being too frightened to send ships. He blamed Roosevelt for "sending troops and guns to a cousin, England, while a daughter, the Philippines, is being raped in a back room."

**FEB. 18:** *New York, Paramount Theater*

The Glenn Miller Orchestra, newly crowned by a disc jockey as "America's Number One Dance Band," began to play its newest hit to teenagers dancing the "Lindy Hop" in the aisles. The song was called "Don't Sit Under the Apple Tree."

**FEB. 19:** *Corregidor*

An American submarine, sent by General Eisenhower, slipped under the Japanese blockade and docked, carrying a few tons of food. Its skipper brought a message from General Marshall: The sub would carry Mrs. MacArthur and her son to safety in Australia some 2,500 miles away.

"No," Jean MacArthur told the sub's commander, she would stay with her husband.

"But what will happen to the boy?"

"We drink," she said, "from the same cup." She and her boy would share her husband's fate.

MacArthur thanked General Marshall for

the offer, sending this cable to Washington: "I and my family will share the fate of the garrison."

**FEB. 22:** *Washington, the White House, the Oval Office*

G eneral Marshall told the President why he wanted to order MacArthur to leave Corregidor and try to escape to Australia. "The Australians and British want one of their own generals to be Supreme Commander in the South Pacific Theater."

Roosevelt did not like MacArthur. They had fought bitterly a few years earlier when MacArthur was Army chief of staff. He knew the Republicans were talking about nominating MacArthur as their candidate for president in 1944. But Roosevelt also knew that if MacArthur escaped from doomed Corregidor, Americans would look upon a defeat in the Philippines as a victory. And, Roosevelt knew, Americans desperately needed any kind of victory after almost three months of stunning defeats.

Marshall left the office with an order from the commander in chief to MacArthur: Leave Corregidor for Australia as soon as possible in whatever way you can.

**FEB. 23:** *Corregidor*

M acArthur was finishing his skimpy dinner—he and his family also lived on half rations—when Dick Sutherland handed him a cable from Roosevelt ordering him to leave for Australia.

MacArthur told Sutherland he would not abandon his troops. He said he would disobey the order, resign as a general, then join the infantry on Bataan "as a simple volunteer."

Sutherland said quietly, "You are needed in Australia far more than you are needed on Bataan."

MacArthur told Sutherland to delay replying to the order while he decided what to do.

**FEB. 24:** *Washington, the White House broadcast studio, 9:45 P.M., Eastern Standard Time*

The grinning President waved to the guests, who stood and clapped politely as he was wheeled to the row of microphones. They were here to watch Roosevelt deliver a speech broadcast by radio to the nation. He had promised to tell "just where we stand in the war." Theaters were interrupting movies and hooking up their loudspeakers so that audiences could hear the speech.

**FEB. 24:** *Washington, the White House broadcast studio, 10:05 P.M., Eastern Standard Time*

"This war is a new kind of war," the President was telling the nation. "It is warfare on every continent, every island, every sea, every ocean in the world." With his mellow, reassuring, fatherly voice, he told anxious

Americans, ears close to their living room radios: "We have most certainly suffered losses—from Hitler's U-boats in the Atlantic and from the Japanese in the Pacific—and we shall suffer more of them before the turn of the tide."

". . . before the turn of the tide." He said those words with a certainty in his voice that made his guests nod to one another: "Yes, the tide is running against us now, but America will turn the tide."

**FEB. 24:** *Goleta, California, eight miles north of Santa Barbara, 7:10 P.M., Pacific Standard Time*

Larry Wheeler and his wife were listening to the President's speech on the radio when they heard a distant explosion. Then came a second—closer. The third rattled pictures on the walls of their house near the Ellwood oil fields.

They ran out into the twilight and heard an object whiz over their heads. A twenty-foot-high column of dirt fountained into the air from the wall of a cliff. Wheeler shouted above the roar of the explosion, "Someone's shooting at us!"

A neighbor, George Brown, ran to the edge of Highway 101 and looked down at Santa Barbara Channel. He saw a submarine sitting flat in the channel. Three men on deck crouched behind a gun. "I've seen American submarines," he said later, "but this was the biggest sub I ever saw. I thought it was a destroyer."

As Brown watched, the Japanese submarine fired fifteen shells that roared into the empty oil fields. One blew apart a derrick; the others threw up showers of dirt.

The gunners took apart the gun, opened a hatch in the sub's tower, and dropped below, one by one. The sub sat silently in the channel until darkness came, and Brown could see it no longer. By now Wheeler had phoned the police to tell them that a Japanese gun was pouring shells into the state of California.

**FEB. 28:** *Aboard the U.S. destroyer* Jacob Jones *off Cape May, New Jersey*

Joe Tidwell, a twenty-two-year-old sailor, came off his watch at 4:55 A.M. and went to the galley for coffee. He stared out a porthole at a dark and blustery ocean flecked with whitecaps. The deck of the galley suddenly lifted up, and Joe reeled backward, hitting the wall. Pots and pans showered down on him. He felt the ship heel sharply to its port side.

Tidwell ran up on deck, hearing an officer shout, "Torpedo amidships, all hands abandon ship!"

Tidwell and another sailor cut loose a raft. They threw it into the water, then dived in after it. The thirty-eight-degree water cut through Tidwell's peacoat, numbing his body. Other sailors clutched at rafts, shouting for help. Tidwell saw the ship's bow crack wide open. Then the *Jakie,* as the crew called the destroyer, blew up, the ocean heaving upward, tossing swimmers like popping popcorn.

Tidwell and ten others of the *Jakie* crew were picked up at noon. They were the only survivors of the 122-man crew of the first warship ever torpedoed in U.S. coastal waters. The *Jakie* was the twenty-third ship sunk off the East Coast in two months, with the death toll now at 568.

# Chapter Three

**MARCH 10:** *Corregidor, Malinta Tunnel*

The acrid smell of dust and gunpowder filled the tunnel as tall, sunken-cheeked General Jonathan Wainwright and General MacArthur sat facing each other in Mac-Arthur's rock-walled office. MacArthur had called "Skinny" Wainwright over from Bataan. He told Wainwright he had decided to obey Roosevelt's order and go to Australia. Wainwright would take command of the trapped army on Bataan and Corregidor.

"If I get through to Australia," MacArthur told Wainwright, "you know I'll come back as soon as I can with as much as I can. In the meantime, you've got to hold."

**MARCH 11:** *Corregidor*

Bursting shells lit up the night sky above the hills of Bataan as MacArthur, his wife, little Arthur, Arthur's nurse, Dick Sutherland, and seventeen other officers walked to a dock. MacArthur had decided to board a PT (Patrol-Torpedo) boat to try to slip through the Japanese ships that ringed the Philippines. The PT boat, he hoped, could get him to the Philippine island of Mindanao some 600 miles away. There a B-17 would try to pick up the MacArthur party and fly them the 2,500 miles to Australia.

The sixty-foot-long wooden PT boats were powered by huge airplane engines. They had streaked around Manila Bay to torpedo a half-dozen Japanese warships. Now MacArthur, his wife, and son were helped onto the tossing *PT-41* by its skipper, Lieutenant John Bulkeley.

MacArthur crouched down in the low-slung, slender boat. "You may cast off, Buck," he said, "when you are ready."

Minutes later *PT-41* led a diamond formation of four PT boats streaking toward the dark and stormy China Sea that was crisscrossed by Japanese subs, ships, and planes.

**MARCH 12:** *Tokyo, Japan, the Diet (Parliament)*

P remier Hideki Tojo was greeted by waves of applause as he stepped to the rostrum. He was reporting to the lawmakers on "the astounding success of our Imperial forces."

So far, he claimed, Japan's army had captured more than 200,000 British and American soldiers. It had shot down or destroyed 1,600 enemy planes. The navy had sunk or damaged seven Allied battleships, three carriers, twelve cruisers, and twenty-two destroyers.

The Japanese soldiers and sailors had carried the flag of the Rising Sun as far east as Wake

Island, 2,000 miles from Tokyo. The flag flew as far west as Singapore in Malaya and Rangoon in Burma, 3,000 miles from Tokyo. To the south, almost 3,000 miles from Tokyo, its troops had conquered Java and the other island nations of the Dutch East Indies. Its troops marched through the dusty streets of Saigon and Hanoi in French Indochina. Its navy had landed troops in the Solomon, Gilbert, Caroline, and Marshall islands in the southwest Pacific, some as far as 3,000 miles from Tokyo and only 1,500 miles from Hawaii. From those island bases—they included places like Truk, Rabaul, and Guadalcanal—Japan could sink ships carrying help to besieged Australia and New Zealand.

As the Diet members cheered, Tojo told of landings by Japan's troops on New Guinea, a mountainous jungle island on the doorstep of Australia. One more thrust of Japan's sword, Tojo said, and India and Australia would fall. Japan would stand tall over all of Asia, one foot on India in the west, one foot on Australia in the east.

"I say to India, Australia and China," Tojo shouted, "lay down your arms because you can no longer defend yourself against our invincible forces."

**MARCH 12:** *The China Sea, off the Philippines*
*P*T-41 bounced and banged against mountainous ocean waves, its engines roaring. Below deck General MacArthur and his small

boy retched together, their faces white with seasickness, as ocean spray drenched their clothes.

*PT-41* had come about halfway toward Mindanao. The sun had set, and a misty fog shrouded the white-capped Pacific.

Standing at the wheel, Lieutenant Bulkeley suddenly cut his engines. MacArthur stood up and saw a Japanese cruiser sliding across the gray ocean only 800 yards away.

Bulkeley ordered quiet. Mrs. MacArthur cradled Arthur in her arms. If one Japanese lookout picked up binoculars, Japan would capture the only general who had slowed its sweeping tide.

**MARCH 17:** *Alice Springs, Australia*

The B-17 Flying Fortress thumped down onto the runway and rolled to a stop. From its door stepped General MacArthur, Jean Mac-Arthur, and a grinning Arthur, who clutched a felt bunny rabbit stiffened by drenchings of ocean water.

*PT-41* had slipped past the Japanese cruiser and sped to Mindanao. From there the B-17 had outraced pursuing Japanese fighters and carried the MacArthurs to Australia.

**MARCH 21:** *Washington, the White House, the Oval Office*

A news reporter asked the President why the Navy could not sink at least one of those subs that had attacked ships within a few miles of the East and West Coasts. Torpedoed ships were going down at the rate of almost one a day. Almost 1,000 seamen had been killed.

The Navy did not own enough destroyers to cover all those thousands of miles of water, the President replied. In fact, he added, "an enemy ship could swoop in and shell New York. Enemy planes could bomb Manhattan. Enemy planes could drop bombs on war plants in Detroit. Enemy troops could attack Alaska."

"Aren't the Army and Navy strong enough to deal with anything like that?" asked a reporter.

"Certainly not," said the commander in chief.

**MARCH 21:** *Adelaide, Australia*

MacArthur met with reporters and told them: "The President of the United States ordered me to break through the Japanese lines and proceed from Corregidor to Australia." He was here, he said, to throw a counterpunch at the Japanese tide. He was also here, he said, to take back the Philippines. "I came through," he said in his stern voice, "and I shall return."

**MARCH 21:** *Manila, Philippines, Japanese army headquarters*

His bald head gleaming in the humid heat, General Tomoyuki Yamashita—the conqueror of Malaya and Singapore—entered the room. Two dozen generals snapped to attention. In Tokyo, admirals were fuming that their battleships could not refuel and repair in Manila Bay because the Americans held the guns of Corregidor. The Japanese had counted on capturing the Philippines in forty days. The American and Filipino soldiers had held out for more than 100 days.

Fresh troops—some 20,000—would reinforce the 40,000 Japanese on Bataan, Yamashita told the generals, including General Masaharu Homma, whom he was replacing. In ten days, said the Tiger of Malaya, the final offensive would begin to push the Bataan defenders into the sea.

**MARCH 21:** *Aboard a train bound for Melbourne, Australia*

An American officer was giving MacArthur and his chief of staff, Dick Sutherland, a briefing on the military situation in and around Australia. With them was American war correspondent Clark Lee, who had escaped from Bataan. While on Corregidor MacArthur had heard a short-wave radio broadcast telling of a "mighty United States force, its hundreds of ships packed to the gunwales with guns, tanks, planes and troops, steaming toward Australia."

The officer told MacArthur that the Japanese were using Truk, Rabaul, and Guadalcanal as bases to bomb Australian cities. And, he added, the Japanese invaders on New Guinea were advancing swiftly toward Port Moresby, which could be a jumping-off base for an invasion of Australia, only a few hundred miles away. In Melbourne, which would be MacArthur's headquarters, trenches were being dug in public parks and air-raid shelters built in the middle of the city. Prime Minister John Curtin had warned that "an invasion by Japan's army is imminent."

MacArthur interrupted to ask when all those troops, tanks, planes, and ships had arrived from America.

"There are very few troops, tanks or planes in Australia, sir," said the officer, adding that most of the Australian and New Zealand troops were fighting with the Eighth Army in North Africa.

"How many troops are there?"

"About 25,000, sir."

MacArthur had left almost three times that many on little Bataan. Now he had to defend an entire continent with 25,000 men. Clark Lee saw MacArthur's face. "It turned deathly white," Lee wrote in his diary, "and his lips twitched."

"Surely he is wrong," MacArthur said to Sutherland.

But MacArthur knew the officer was right. "It was the biggest damned surprise of the war," he said later to Clark Lee. He looked out the window of the train at the passing Australian prairie and murmured, "Let God have mercy on us."

**MARCH 22:** *Chungking, China*

Colonel Frank Dorn, blue-eyed and built like a football tackle, had just arrived with his boss, Lieutenant General Joseph "Vinegar Joe" Stilwell. A spare, stooped U.S. Army veteran of the Spanish-American War, the grizzled Stilwell had been stationed in China when the Japanese invaded in 1937. He had watched the Japanese sweep the Nationalist armies of Chiang Kai-shek out of the coastal cities of Peking, Shanghai, and Hong Kong. Chiang Kai-shek had retreated deep into China to this dusty, crowded city on a mountain near French Indochina and Burma. He and his Chinese Communist ally, Mao Tse-tung, had more men than the Japanese—millions more. But China had no planes and only a handful of tanks. Japanese tanks squashed Chinese peasant soldiers firing bullets that pinged off the steel tanks. With tons of bombs, Japanese planes bombed and strafed Chungking and other cities held by Chiang and Mao as soldiers and civilians huddled in caves.

General Marshall had sent Stilwell and Dorn to China. Their mission: to use American tanks and planes to build up the Chinese armies so they could push the Japanese back to the coast. From the China coast, a United Nations army could cross the Sea of Japan to invade Japan's island fortress.

Their mission was next to impossible, Dorn and Stilwell now realized, because Chiang Kai-shek guarded his power so jealously that he would not let Stilwell give orders to his warload generals. Those warlords, Dorn and Stilwell knew, extorted money from rich and poor Chinese and took bribes from the Japanese. They wanted the war to go on without victory for any side. Dorn suspected that the Gissimo, as Generalissimo Chiang liked to call himself, was also making millions out of the war.

Colonel Dorn had winced when he saw Chungking, Chiang Kai-shek's capital. It hung on a cliff between two rivers. "Chungking," he wrote, "was steeped in gloomy dampness and rife with the stench of rotting food, filth and human excreta. It was jammed with soldiers and refugees."

He talked to the soldiers. One told him: "The Chinese soldier does not fear death. But he dreads a crippling wound because he will be left to bleed and die on the battlefield without water, food or care."

Warlords hired the soldiers for a penny or two a day. The soldiers were peasants eager to escape the brutal harshness of a slavelike life in rice paddies. Civilians lived in fear of the secret police thugs hired by Chiang. Chiang Kai-shek ruled China with a hand as iron as Stalin's or Hitler's.

Colonel Dorn visited a tungsten mine owned by one of Chiang's chief generals. Ten-year-old boys and girls had to squeeze on hands and knees through narrow, dark tunnels that were too narrow for adult miners. The children were sold to the mine's owners by starving parents. Whimpering for parents they would never see again, the children worked twelve to fourteen hours a day in the dark mines. They were starved to keep them from growing. After a year, they died and were replaced by fresh batches of wide-eyed, frightened ten-year-olds.

Ever since his arrival two months earlier, General Stilwell had tried to get rid of corrupt generals in the Chinese army. Stilwell wanted generals who would push back the Japanese instead of crouching in mountainous hideouts and sniping at Japanese patrols in meaningless skirmishes.

The mustached Gissimo listened with a polite smile. Sitting next to him was his wife, a queenlike woman known as Madame Chiang. A dark-haired, doll-faced former movie actress, Madame Chiang came from a family of rich Shanghai bankers. (The Gissimo was the son of peasants.) She and the Gissimo bickered constantly, the Chinese told Dorn, and the Gissimo had twice left her with a black eye. But they needed each other. He needed the money of her rich relatives, including her uncle, T. V. Soong, China's Ambasssador to the United States. And she and her family needed Chiang's soldiers and secret police.

A Chinese army had gone to British-owned Burma, about 500 miles from China, to fight the invading Japanese alongside a British army. The British and Chinese were retreating to north Burma, hammered by the advancing Japanese. The port of Rangoon, in south Burma, had fallen to the Japanese.

"If the Japanese capture Mandalay in north Burma," Stilwell told Chiang, "they will cut off your supplies coming from America." He pleaded with Chiang: "Let me take command of the Chinese Sixth Army in Burma so we can hold Mandalay and recapture Rangoon." From Rangoon, trucks carried weapons to China on the Burma Road, a thousand-mile road that snaked up and around the Himalayan Mountains to Chungking. American pilots called the Flying Tigers were now carrying American guns and supplies to Chungking by flying across the Himalayas, known as the Hump.

Chiang knew he needed the Burma Road— and Americans like Stilwell—for his own survival. Finally, he agreed to the plan. Stilwell and Dorn took off in a plane to fly across the Hump and try to save Burma.

**MARCH 23:** *Pasadena, California, the Rose Bowl parking lot*

At dawn the jalopies and trucks, filled with washing machines, suitcases, furniture, and other possessions, began to line up outside the famous football stadium. The cars and trucks, some wheezing and sputtering, were filled with Japanese-American families. They had volunteered to leave coastal areas for a camp that had been hastily built in Owens Val-

A Japanese family lines up to leave their home in Hayward, California, and be evacuated to a camp in the interior of the state. They are wearing identification tags to ensure that the family will not be separated. At the camps the evacuees were assigned jobs like building roads and houses, running stores, and growing crops. They were paid by the U.S. government, part of their pay going for their food and housing. Almost fifty years later the U.S. government gave many of these evacuated people, or their descendants, money to pay them back for income lost because of the forced evacuation—the largest one in American history. *(Photo courtesy of the National Archives)*

ley, an eight-hour drive away. Owens Valley would be one of a dozen areas receiving 100,000 Japanese, citizens and aliens. They would be dispersed in camps across the interiors of California, Oregon, Washington, Idaho, Colorado, and Arizona.

At 9:00 A.M. the first cars rolled out of the parking lot, led by wailing police cars and escorted by Army soldiers in trucks and jeeps. What newspapers were calling "the greatest forced migration in U.S. history" had begun.

One evacuee was Mike Nishida, twenty-one, a Nisei (American-born Japanese) who was being drafted into the Army a month from now. "I'm going up there in the valley to do any job they want me to do before I go into service," he said.

**MARCH 23:** *Manzanar, Owens Valley, California*

The Japanese-Americans were marched to barracks by military policemen who towered over them. One Japanese man, an American citizen, told a reporter for the *San Francisco Chronicle:* "We come here without bitterness or rancor, but only as a people wanting to show our loyalty in deeds, not words."

Women stared impassively as MPs rummaged through clothes in suitcases to be sure the Japanese brought with them no short-wave radios, weapons, or signal flares.

One reporter, Neil Naden, watched the evacuees filing silently into their barracks. "They're cooperative, cheerful, and homesick," he wrote later. "If they are also heartsick, you can't tell."

The Japanese would earn $50 to $94 a month in the camps working on government projects, said General John DeWitt. Fifteen dollars would be deducted for each person's room and board. No one, said the General, was allowed to leave the camp without permission. "They have forfeited their freedom for the duration," said another officer. On April 1 the evacuations would no longer be voluntary. "If families are forced to evacuate," said General DeWitt, "the moving from their homes will be much harder than if they volunteer to leave."

**MARCH 31:** *San Francisco, a booth in a restaurant*

The four Army and Navy officers wore civilian clothes so they would not be noticed. The chesty Admiral Bill Halsey stared across the table at the moon-faced, slouching Jimmy Doolittle, a former racing and stunt pilot. Now forty-five, Doolittle was a colonel in the Army Air Corps and had been personally picked by General Marshall and President Roosevelt to try to score the first victory of the war. His orders: Bomb Tokyo.

Only an aircraft carrier could get close enough to Japan for Doolittle's B-25 bombers to reach Tokyo. But could a big B-25 get into the air off the short runway of an aircraft carrier as it plunged through the ocean? Or would it fall into the sea? Doolittle had picked a band of almost a hundred volunteer flyers willing to risk their lives to find out.

"We will carry your sixteen bombers within 400 miles of Tokyo, if we can sneak in that close," Admiral Halsey told Doolittle. "But if the Japanese spot us, we will have to launch you sooner, but only if you are close enough to reach Tokyo."

"That suits me," Dootlittle said. He knew that the bombers' tanks would run dry after they crossed Japan. They hoped to land in China where, they also hoped, the troops of Chiang Kai-shek would get them to safety.

Halsey and Doolittle shook hands and left the restaurant. Their next date would be in the Pacific as close to Tokyo as they could get.

Chapter Four

**APRIL 1:** *Philadelphia, Pennsylvania*

A bridal adviser suggested that if a bride were marrying a man in Army khaki or Navy blue, "consider wearing shell pink or hyacinth blue instead of the traditional white. Those colors make a gay complement to khaki or navy."

**APRIL 2:** *San Francisco Bay*

The carrier *Hornet* slipped through the dusk under the Golden Gate Bridge, gliding into the Pacific, where she would rendezvous with the task force of battleships, cruisers, and destroyers commanded by Admiral Bill Halsey. On board the *Hornet* were Jimmy Doolittle's sixteen B-25s and their crews. Their destination, Tokyo.

**APRIL 3:** *Near the Colorado River in Arizona*

Major General George Patton took command of two 8,000-man tank battalions and announced they were the nucleus of the new First Armored Corps. Riding atop the turret of his personal tank, decorated with the two stars of his rank, Patton led columns of new tanks and armored cars across the desert in mock battles. At night he slept by the side of his tank, a pearl-handled pistol strapped to his side. He told his officers they were training to fight Hitler's Panzers on the deserts of North Africa—perhaps as early as that summer.

"We have the best tanks in the world," Patton told his young officers. He had driven French tanks in World War I and helped design the first American-built tanks. "But you don't win wars with machines," he said. "You win wars with guts."

His officers began to call the fifty-seven-year-old Patton Old Blood and Guts.

**APRIL 4:** *Wolf's Lair, Hitler's Russian headquarters in eastern Germany*

Joseph Goebbels, Hitler's scrawny propaganda chief, had not seen Hitler in two months. Goebbels's jaw dropped when he saw that the fifty-three-year-old Hitler's hair had turned almost entirely gray during the past winter. Hitler told Goebbels, "I have to fight off severe attacks of giddiness."

Hitler had fled his winter home at Berchtesgaden. He had always loved to stare out at the snow-covered mountains. Now, he told Goebbels, even a glance at snow or ice made him want to throw up. "It worries and torments me," Hitler said, "that that country"—he meant Russia—"is still covered with snow."

Hitler knew he had to rest and reinforce his armies in Russia for a summer offensive. Of 162 divisions that had invaded Russia, only eight had enough soldiers fit for combat. And of more than 10,000 tanks that had begun the war, only 140 were capable of fighting.

Hitler told Goebbels he would begin to draft into the army German men as young as sixteen and as old as fifty. He would force his allies—Rumania, Italy, Bulgaria—into sending forty fresh divisions. And his war-production wizard, the crafty Albert Speer, had promised him 1,000 new tanks for the summer offensive. But he needed oil for the engines. His primary target, he told Goebbels, would be the oil fields of the Caucasus in southern Russia. "If I do not get the oil," he told Goebbels, "then I must end this war."

If his armies grabbed the Caucasian oil, he said, "Russia's sources of oil are exhausted and she will be brought to her knees. Then the British . . . will surrender in order to save what remains of the Empire. America is a big bluff."

Hitler sent a message to General Friedrich von Paulus, commander of his Sixth Army, which would start the summer offense, reminding him that the key to the oil fields lay in capturing the city of Stalingrad. Take Stalingrad from the Russians, Hitler said, and the Germans would cut Stalin's fuel lines.

**APRIL 4:** *Bataan, the Bagac-Onon Defensive Line*

No longer did GIs climb trees to look for the masts of a rescuing task force. The sick and starving men of Bataan, their clothes flapping on their sticklike legs and arms, knew that no help was coming. At night they sang this angry song: "We are the Battlin' Bastards of Bataan,/No momma, no poppa, no Uncle Sam."

Nearly all of the 85,000 American and Filipino survivors on Bataan and Corregidor shivered sometimes uncontrollably as malarial fever swept over their starved bodies. Doctors had no more drugs to fight the malaria. Almost 10,000 men writhed on cots in field hospitals, their wounds now pus-filled and gangrenous. Others retched with beriberi and other killing jungle diseases carried by the swarms of flies that fed on rotting corpses.

Twelve GIs shared one can of salmon a day. At dusk they hunted on their hands and knees for lizards and monkeys. They cooked pots of rice that tasted, said one soldier, "like paper paste."

The GIs had lived in smelly, slimy foxholes in the jungle for two months. Each day, under the blazing sun, they ducked whizzing bullets. At night they dozed, waking every few minutes at the sound of a twig cracking.

They talked about their dreams. "If I ever

**BY DOING THIS**

He got his food.

He got his cigs.

Above all, he's assured of life and the chance to get back home --

The Japanese tried to lure Americans on Bataan into surrendering by dropping propaganda leaflets like this behind the American lines. The Americans were not fooled by the promise to get back home. *(Photo originally appeared in* The Washington Post; *reprinted by permission of the D.C. Public Library)*

hit San Francisco," one told another, "I'll walk into the best restaurant and order salmon. When the waiter brings it to my table, I'll throw that plate of salmon on the floor and order the thickest T-bone steak they got."

The GIs knew that the Japanese were massing for one final drive. They could hear the rumble and roar of Japanese tanks cracking through jungle clearings.

Colonel Ernie Miller had gathered the remnants of his tank battalion for a final stand. "The Japs won't beat us," he told his troops. "But what is beating us is disease and hunger."

**APRIL 7:** *Washington, the Navy Department*

M aking what he called "a historic change," Secretary of the Navy Frank Knox announced that "all Negro volunteers will be offered jobs other than their traditional ones in the Navy—cooks, stewards, and mess boys. They will be given combat jobs and in fact there may even be a destroyer that is all Negro except for officers. It is not contemplated at present that there will be Negro Navy officers."

**APRIL 9–13:** *Bataan*

H is tankers stood silent in the dusk as Colonel Ernie Miller told them that Bataan's commanding general had surrendered all the 75,000 troops on Bataan. General Wainwright, he said, had escaped to Corregidor, where a small band of about 10,000 would make a last stand.

Colonel Miller told his men to break open their last cans of food, treats that had been saved for a "victory celebration." The men licked their lips as they gulped down peaches and corned beef hash. Then they slept soundly for the first time in weeks.

The next morning the Japanese troops came down the narrow trails. They told Colonel Miller and his men to stack their weapons. But the Japanese would get no Made in America tanks. The Americans had blown them up.

One English-speaking officer told Miller, "You fight bravely. But you should never have surrendered."

"We were too weak to fight any longer."

"Japanese do not surrender," the officer said. Miller's tankers had captured more than 400 Japanese in the last two months, but he said nothing.

Miller asked about food for his men. The

Grim-faced Americans captured after the fall of Bataan march with hands upraised and guarded by triumphant Japanese soldiers. This was the start of the Bataan Death March that killed thousands of American and Filipino soldiers. The Japanese were especially cruel to the Filipinos. The Japanese had expected that their fellow Asians would cross over to their side after the invasion of the Philippines, but most Filipinos stayed loyal to the United States. *(Photo courtesy of the National Archives)*

officer said the Japanese had only enough rice and dried fish for themselves.

Flanked by the grinning Japanese troops, Miller and his men began to march under the glaring sun toward prison camps that the officer said were about 100 miles away. The weary, stumbling column of Americans came out of the jungle onto a long, dusty road. Trucks sped by, carrying Japanese soldiers. They jeered at the staggering, scarecrow-thin Americans, swinging at the prisoners with their rifle butts.

At noon the Japanese ordered the Americans to sit in the sun while the Japanese ate and drank. The Americans got no food, only a few drops of water. The march began again. Americans collapsed. The Japanese beat each fallen GI with a rifle until the man stood up and fell into line, supported by his comrades. If a prisoner did not rise, a Japanese soldier ran at him and plunged a bayonet into his belly. Colonel Miller trudged through the dust, hearing the shrieks and moans of dying Americans.

As they marched, Colonel Miller and his men saw the bodies of Americans and Filipino soldiers who had come this way before them. Some bodies had been nailed to posts, then bayoneted savagely. The crucified corpses were grisly warnings to the prisoners to keep moving no matter how painful it was.

Near evening Miller and his men were crammed into barbed-wire pens. They had to sit under the eyes of Japanese guards. Each prisoner got four spoons of rice and a little water.

Earlier prisoners had dug large pits in the middle of the pens for use as toilets. Thousands of Americans and Filipinos had used the pits, which now overflowed. The suffocating stench made Miller gag. Miller watched men begin to babble deliriously. Other keeled over, their bodies shaking with fever. By morning dozens were open-eyed corpses.

The prisoners marched all morning in the blazing heat. Then they were crammed into railroad boxcars—110 men in a car that could hold no more than fifty. The men had to stand or sit. No one could move more than a few inches. Guards slammed shut the doors, and the heat inside was oven-hot.

Three hours later the dazed Americans toppled out of the cars, leaving behind their dead. They marched another two days, beaten and bayoneted all the way.

Miller survived one beating that broke bones in his jaw. He staggered into Camp McDonnell, the last stop for the survivors. Many other Filipinos and Americans, who had been force-marched thirteen days by the Japanese, fell in the camp's dust and were buried the next day in mass graves.

During the next few weeks Miller learned that of 75,000 men who had surrendered on Bataan—12,000 of them Americans—about 7,800 Filipinos and 2,300 Americans had died on what would be called the Bataan Death March.

At Camp McDonnell the survivors got only a little food and water. Prisoners who could not move were beaten, shot, or bayoneted. "We had called it Camp McDonnell before the march," Miller would one day write. "We had been there only a few days when we called it Camp Death."

In factories and shipyards, proud employees put up Service Star posters to show how many of their fellow workers had gone to war. This Manhattan fish-market worker is posed in front of a Service Star poster boasting of its first WAAC and its 170 men "serving our country." *(Photo courtesy of The Library of Congress)*

**APRIL 17:** *Aboard the* Hornet *in the Pacific, about 900 miles from Tokyo*

Japanese fishing boats had spotted Task Force 6, Admiral Bill Halsey's force carrying Jimmy Doolittle's bombers. Halsey radioed Doolittle from his carrier, the *Enterprise,* that he dare come no closer than 800 miles of Japan. He feared he would be trapped. Doolittle's bombers had to take off for Japan within the next twenty-four hours.

**APRIL 18:** *The White House, the Oval office*

The President scanned the long sheets of paper. This was America's first casualty list of World War II, the names of more than 30,000 soldiers, sailors, and marines killed, wounded, missing, or captured since December 7. Mothers and wives and children were receiving tele-

One of Colonel Jimmy Doolittle's B-25 bombers takes off from the deck of the *Hornet*, bound for Japan and the bombing of Tokyo. Top American admirals and generals opposed sending a large task force for a raid that they knew would do no damage to Japan's military might. But Roosevelt insisted on the raid to boost the morale of the American people. *(Photo courtesy of the National Archives)*

grams that began, "We regret to inform you that . . ." Roosevelt was writing a speech to be made on radio to the American people. He added a new sentence to the speech: "The price of civilization must be paid in hard work and sorrow and blood."

**APRIL 18:** *Flight deck of the* Hornet *in the Pacific, about 800 miles from Japan*

Jimmy Doolittle's B-25 rumbled down the deck toward the tossing ocean and the white wake of the carrier. The fifteen other pilots craned their necks from their cockpits to watch the takeoff with anxious eyes.

He's going too slow, navigator Carl Wildner told himself. He won't make it.

Doolittle's plane roared within yards of the

deck's yawning edge. Wildner saw a gap of light between the plane's wheels and the deck. The husky bomber lifted off into the shimmering blue sky.

Fear churned inside Wildner's stomach as his pilot, Travis Hoover, shot his plane toward the abyss at the deck's end. "I braced myself for the crash I felt was coming," he later wrote. "I was sure we were going right off the end into the dirty green water. . . . I'll admit I was scared."

Pulling the wheel upward against his chest, the pilot lifted the bomber. It skimmed over the water and soared toward the sun.

One by one the other B-25s took off from the carrier, turned lazy circles toward the west, then set courses for Tokyo, Yokohama, Nagoya, Yokosuka, Kobe—and a safe landing, they hoped, in faraway China.

**APRIL 18:** *100 feet over Japan*

Jimmy Doolittle gripped the controls and watched the housetops flash by below him. He had been flying for almost five hours. Travis Hoover's B-25 flew at his wing tip.

People had heard their oncoming roar. They stood in roads, waving, thinking they were Japanese planes. Then they saw the red, white, and blue stars on the wings. One boy leaped from his bicycle and dived into a ditch.

Doolittle looked up and saw nine Japanese pursuit planes high above them. The two

American bombers, flying at 300 miles an hour, whizzed too close the ground to be spotted from that high up.

Tokyo loomed ahead. It was a little after noon, Tokyo time. Doolittle pulled back on the wheel and climbed to 1,200 feet. He carried incendiary bombs meant for a row of wooden factories.

Black puffs flared all around the bomber, shaking the plane. Bits of flak tore holes in the tail.

Open the bomb bay, Doolittle told bombardier Sergeant Fred Braemer.

The bomb-bay doors slid open. Braemer stared down the bomb sight and watched the factories come between the cross hairs of the sight. He flicked a switch, and the first American bombs of World War II began to fall on the people of Japan.

**APRIL 18:** *Tokyo city center*

Crowds jammed rooftops, screaming with excitement as the planes roared overhead. People thought they were watching an air-raid drill made as realistic as possible by their aviators.

Thick columns of smoke mushroomed upward from the factories, tongues of flames licking into the smoke. Faces turned white with shock as men, women, and children looked up for the first time at an enemy aiming to kill them.

Thirteen-year-old Toshika Yuruku watched

from her rooftop. "We finally began to realize that what our elders and the government had told us—that we could never be attacked—was not true," she wrote in her diary that night. "We had been told that Japan could never be conquered. Now we began to doubt that we could never be conquered."

## APRIL 18: *500 feet over a Tokyo suburb*

Brown fields flew by below Jimmy Doolittle's bomber as it winged westward. The two lead B-25s were being followed across Tokyo by eight other B-25s. The other six bombers streaked toward Yokohama, Nagoya, and Kobe.

Doolittle glanced at his dropping fuel gauges. He had to stay aloft another nine to ten hours to reach the coast of China.

## APRIL 18: *Toungoo, Burma*

Lanky twenty-three-year-old Duke Hedman smiled as Colonel Claire Chennault shook his hand. Earlier today, Duke had gunned down five Japanese planes.

Colonel Claire Chennault commanded the American Volunteer Group (AVG), 100 or so American flyers. The leathery-faced Chennault had retired as an Army flyer because of deafness. He had joined Chiang Kai-shek's army as an unofficial chief of China's air corps, teaching young pilots how to win dogfights in their beat-up old planes.

In 1941 Chennault went to Washington. He talked to President Roosevelt. "You're sending Lend-Lease guns and other weapons to the Chinese," he said. "But most never get there."

Ships had to dock the weapons in south Burma. Trucks carried them into China on the Burma Road. Japanese bombers blew up the trucks. Chennault talked Roosevelt into sending to China about 100 old P-40 Tomahawk fighter planes to ward off the Japanese planes. Roosevelt also allowed American Army fighter pilots to join Chennault's new American Volunteer Group. AVG pilots got $600 a month plus a $500 bonus for each plane they shot down.

Claire Chennault taught them all he knew about dealing out death in the sky. "Fight always in pairs," he told them. "The lead plane goes in for the kill. The wing man protects his tail. It's like boxing—your left hand attacks, the right hand defends. The Zeros are the world's best fighters. They climb faster and are quicker in a dive than the P-40s. Climb only when you are safe from the Zero's guns, or that Zero will trace holes in your belly. Don't forget that— your lives depend on it."

Reporters soon dubbed Chennault's aces the Flying Tigers. Flying from dusty, windswept airdromes in Burma and China, the Flying Tigers had shot down at least 250 Japanese planes and killed more than 1,200 of Japan's best pilots. The Tigers had lost only twenty planes and a dozen pilots.

Duke Hedman had flown this afternoon with squadron leader Gregory ("Pappy") Boyington, an "old man" at thirty-five. Duke and Pappy attacked an armada of fifty Mitsubishi bombers droning toward the British and Chinese armies. The troops were retreating north from Rangoon on the road to Mandalay in north Burma.

At 18,000 feet, the jungle below a mass of green, Duke dived his P-40, blasting away at Mitsubishis. A Zero swerved and blasted slugs that tore away the plexiglas canopy over Duke's helmet. Duke's slugs tore into a bomber. It quivered, then exploded, cartwheeling downward. White parachutes bloomed from its broken tail.

Duke swerved out of his dive, catching two Zeros by their tails. Within seconds he blew both away.

He turned and climbed. He saw the needle on his fuel gauge swing wildly toward empty. Bullets had ripped a hole in his fuel tank. But Duke curved his fighter to face the bombers.

"You're crazy!" shouted Pappy Boyington over the radio.

Duke wobbled through the bombers, guns chattering. Another bomber spiraled downward in flames.

Boyington had just landed to tell General Chennault that Duke was dead when Duke came in low over the treetops and set down his riddled Tomahawk on the dusty runway.

**APRIL 18:** *8,000 feet over the China coast*

Doolittle knew his bomber could fly only a few more minutes, its tanks nearly empty after thirteen hours of flight. He told his crew to abandon ship. They buckled on chutes and leapt out of the gliding bomber into the dark moonless night.

**APRIL 20:** *Near Tien Mu Shen, China*

After a day of wandering in a cold rain, Doolittle found his four other crewmen, all uninjured. Friendly Chinese took them to the wreckage of their B-25 sprawled across a mountainside. Doolittle guessed that all sixteen of his bombers had run out of gas and crashed. He wondered if any of the nearly 100 crewmen were still alive.

Doolittle stared at the wreckage, the rain pelting his face. He had never felt lower in his life, trapped and helpless on a landscape as desolate as the moon. A crewman asked, "What do you think will happen when you go home, colonel?"

He would probably be sent to a military prison for this disaster, Doolittle answered.

"No, sir. They'll make you a general. And I bet that they're going to give you the Congressional Medal of Honor."

Doolittle tried to smile. He couldn't.

**APRIL 28:** *Mandalay, Burma*

The broad-brimmed, high-peaked hat made him look like a U.S. forest ranger or some leftover soldier from the Spanish-American war. His bony face was impassive, but his blue eyes glittered angrily. Vinegar Joe Stilwell was watching the retreat toward India of the British and Chinese troops he had hoped to whip into a fighting force to stop the Japanese invasion of Burma. British generals had looked down their noses at this American cowboy who gave them advice on how to stop the Japanese. Chinese generals had ignored him; instead they took orders from Chiang Kai-shek, who was trying to fight the war from nearly 1,000 miles away.

The Japanese jungle fighters swept through and around the bewildered Chinese and British. Japanese planes strafed and dive-bombed these defeated soldiers whenever they paused in their retreat. When they reached the mountains of north Burma, they would have to make a decision; either turn to face certain slaughter, or try to climb those mountains toward India with the Japanese snapping at their heels.

Colonel Dorn watched the exhausted British, "tired English lads, their faces burned red by weeks of scorching sun. Some were asleep in vehicles, too exhausted to care as each sudden stop made them loll and jerk like rag dolls. But most were forced to trudge through the night in the powdery dust."

He saw frightened Chinese who knew that

the Japanese mutilated Chinese prisoners caught out of China. Most Chinese walked without shoes, their bleeding feet turning the dust into red mud. They had marched forty miles this day and would have to walk another forty the next. But, as one American officer said later, "the only ones who dropped by the wayside were the dead."

# Chapter Five

**MAY 4:** *Corregidor, Malinta Tunnel*

L ieutenant Juanita Redmond was one of a dozen nurses who were caring for the sick and wounded in the Rock's underground hospital. She heard the sirens, then the familiar "Planes Overhead!"

The bomb hit near the tunnel to the hospital. It went off next to an ammunition truck. The shock waves knocked Redmond to the floor. She rose groggily, seeing bottles of scarce medicine smashed on the rocky floor. She grabbed half-broken bottles, trying to save what she could.

Stretcher bearers came down the dust-filled tunnel carrying shrieking wounded. Redmond ran from bed to bed, cutting traction ropes. If a bomb hit, patients could roll for cover, even though they might crack their broken bones.

Amid the screams, she said later, "it was all I could do to try being calm and acting as if everything were all right."

She heard the sharp whistle of a falling aerial bomb. A sergeant pulled her under a desk. For several heart-pounding moments she could do nothing but wait—"that was the awful part, we couldn't do anything."

The bomb hit the Rock directly above them. The blast hurled Redmond, the sergeant, and the desk upward into the air like dolls and furniture in a toy house.

She hit the floor, the desk crashing down on top of her. She was gasping and thought her eyes were being forced out of their sockets. This is the end, she told herself.

Still on the floor, she looked at what was left of the shattered ward. Mangled bodies were strewn under the tangled wreckage of beds. She saw a bloodstained hand sticking out from under a chair. Arms and legs had been torn off, shattered torsos now impossible to identify. Through a hole in the rocky roof, she saw a bloody body dangling in a nearby tree.

Another nurse, Lieutenant Rosemary Hogan, limped from a nearby tunnel. Blood streamed down Hogan's face and shoulders.

"Is it bad, Hogan?" Redmond asked.

"Just a little nose bleed," said Hogan, her face chalk white.

The wounded screamed and moaned, buried under debris and piles of corpses. Medics dug them out. Lieutenant Redmond poured antiseptics into gaping wounds of men who no longer had arms or legs.

When night came and the sirens stopped, she crawled into a foxhole inside a tunnel. Her black and blue arms and legs ached, but she couldn't sleep. She had not eaten in twenty-four hours, but she wasn't hungry.

At dawn she heard the drone of the bombers. "We were like hunted animals," she later wrote, "waiting for the kill, almost hoping it would happen quickly so that the torments of waiting would end. This wasn't a war in which anybody—anybody!—is let off."

**MAY 4:** *Corregidor*

Inside a candle-lit tunnel, Lieutenant General Jonathan Wainwright dictated his last radio message to General Marshall in Washington. Japanese troops swarmed over the island. Bombers shook the Rock. The wounded could no longer be protected. He was surrendering, Wainwright said, "with broken heart . . . but not in shame."

**MAY 5:** *Aboard the world's biggest battleship, the 80,000-ton* Yamato, *off Japan*

Admiral Isoroku Yamamoto smiled as he received the order from Imperial Naval Headquarters, an order he, as the Hero of Pearl Harbor, had demanded. It approved a plan almost as daring as his brilliant plan for the attack on Pearl Harbor.

Yamamoto had reminded Prime Minister Tojo that American planes had just bombed Tokyo. He said the planes would come again unless the American fleet could be pushed back to the West Coast of the United States. That meant capturing Hawaii.

According to Yamamoto's plan, the Japanese would first capture a group of tiny islands in the Pacific halfway between Tokyo and Hawaii. Called Midway, they were held by a small American force of marines, which could easily be overwhelmed. Midway would become Japan's hopping-off base to attack Hawaii.

The American fleet might fight to hold Midway, Yamamoto said, but the American ships would be 2,000 miles from their base at Pearl Harbor, and Japan's battleships and aircraft carriers outnumbered the Americans. The Japanese could win what their admirals had long foreseen as the Great All-Out Battle. The battle would send what was left of the American Pacific Fleet limping back to Los Angeles and San Francisco to defend the United States.

Yamamoto called in his chief air officer, Commander Minoru Genda, and his task force commander, Admiral Chuchi Nagumo. These three had plotted the attack on Pearl Harbor. Now they began to plan for the attack that would capture Midway and then Hawaii.

Some 200 warships would rendezvous near Midway, Yamamoto said. The huge armada — the biggest in history — would arrive near Midway on June 4, and would blast the garrison senseless, blowing away any ships that came to its rescue. On June 7 the armada would pour 5,000 troops onto Midway.

## MAY 5: *Corregidor*

R adio operator Irving Strobing tapped out in Morse code the last words of a defeated garrison. "The jig is up. Everyone is bawling like a baby. They are piling dead and wounded in our tunnel. Arms weak . . . long hours . . . short rations . . . tired. . . . Sign my name and tell my mother how you heard from me."

He and the 7,000 other men and women of Corregidor were taken to Bataan to join Colonel Miller and 75,000 American and Filipino men and women who were prisoners in the death camps.

## MAY 6: *Indaw, Burma*

G eneral Stilwell stood on a truck to bellow at his party of 114 American, British, Chinese, and Burmese soldiers and civilians. They would have to walk out of Burma to India about 150 miles away, he told them. They would have to claw through jungles, cross rivers, climb mountains. They would have to ration food and water. Some were sick or injured, but they would have to march fourteen miles a day— "105 steps a minute," Stilwell told them.

"By the time we get out of here," Vinegar Joe told them, "many of you will hate my guts, but I'll tell you one thing: you'll all get out."

He grabbed a walking stick and at a precise 105 steps a minute, counting them out on his watch, he plunged into the jungle, his ragged band trailing after him.

**MAY 7:** *The Coral Sea, between Australia and New Guinea*

Their bows knifing through heavy seas, the battleships and cruisers of Admiral Frank Fletcher's Task Force 17 steamed southward through the Coral Sea. The code breakers in Hawaii had tipped off Admiral Fletcher that a Japanese invasion fleet was heading for Port Moresby on New Guinea's coast. Port Moresby sat on the doorstep of Australia, only a few hundred miles across the Coral Sea from Australia's northern beaches. Port Moresby would be the jumping-off base for a Japanese invasion of Australia.

At 9:30 A.M. Fletcher's scout planes sighted Japanese ships stretched across the horizon some 200 miles from Task Force 17. Dive bombers shot off the decks of the carriers *Lexington* and *Yorktown,* gleaming torpedoes slung under their fuselages. At the same time, Japanese fighters, bombers, and torpedo planes vaulted off two carriers, the *Shokaku* and *Zuikaku,* to attack the Americans.

For the first time in history, two naval forces battled each other without either being close enough to see the other's ships.

**MAY 7:** *Washington, the Office of Production Management (OPM)*

OPM announced that sugar and gasoline would be rationed. One sugar coupon would entitle a person to buy one pound of sugar every two weeks. One gas coupon would entitle a driver to buy two gallons of gasoline a week.

**MAY 8:** *Aboard the U.S. carrier* Lexington *in the Coral Sea*

Captain Ted Sherman stood on the bridge and watched the stream of Japanese torpedo planes flash toward the *Lexington* like silver daggers. He also saw six ribbons of white streak through the water toward the *Lex*—the wake of torpedoes.

The blunt nose of the huge carrier (as long as a city block) swung wide, trying to dodge those wakes. Two torpedoes knifed into the *Lex*'s port side, knocking sailors off their feet. The *Lex* lurched sharply as water cascaded through holes the size of manhole covers.

Sherman ordered slow speed as crewmen patched the holes. The ship's big pom-pom guns blasted at the oncoming bombers at

The American aircraft carrier *Yorktown* and other American warships blast at Japanese planes during the Battle of Midway. The black puffs are exploding antiaircraft shells. On the left is a burning American ship. *(Photo courtesy of the National Archives)*

point-blank range, swatting one after another out of the sky like clay pigeons. Black puffs of smoke filled the air around the attacking planes.

Four Japanese dive bombers plummeted out of the sky, black sticks tumbling from their bellies. Two bombs hit the flight deck, their blasts blowing men and machines skyward like bowling pins. Captain Sherman sailed against the rail of the bridge, almost toppling overboard. Balls of orange flame ballooned upward, and black smoke billowed across the deck, blinding and choking firefighters.

**MAY 8:** *Aboard the Japanese carrier* Shokaku *in the Coral Sea*

The invasion task force's burly, beetle-browed commander, Chuichi ("King Kong") Hara, frowned with worry as three waves of American torpedo bombers streaked low toward his two carriers. He dictated an order to be signaled to his troop ships lumbering behind him toward Port Moresby. He ordered them to go back to the Solomon Islands and wait until he sunk these two American carriers.

**MAY 8:** *Aboard the* Lexington *in the Coral Sea*

Two explosions in her innards rocked the carrier. Pots and pans flew around the ship's galley. The time was near dusk. All of the carrier's surviving planes had returned, the pilot jabbering excitedly of hits and fires on the two Japanese carriers. They stopped as they heard Captain Sherman give the order in a steady voice: Abandon ship!

More than 200 officers and men had died on the *Lexington*, burned to death or suffocated in the raging fires. Captain Sherman went below to say a farewell to his dead and to be sure that no one alive was left behind.

Then, the last man aboard, he grabbed a rope and slid over the side of the fiery *Lexington,* splashing into the water with more than a thousand of his men. They bounced on small rafts as destroyers circled to fish them out.

"She's a tough old lady," Ensign Frank Gill later told a friend. "After we left her, she stood there for four or five hours with a raging inferno eating her out. And still she wouldn't go down. She was like a live thing, trying to make it to port."

Most of the crew were crying as they watched from other ships as an American torpedo finally sank the *Lex*.

**MAY 8:** *Aboard the* Yamoto, *off Japan*

Admiral Yamamoto could hear his staff cheering in the next cabin. Radio messages from the Coral Sea reported that the *Lexington* had gone under and the *Yorktown* was badly damaged. The Japanese had lost only one small carrier. But the two big carriers, *Zuikaku* and *Shokaku,* were crawling back to Japan, the *Zuikaku* almost capsizing on the way. The flight decks of both carriers stretched like empty parking lots. Almost 100 of their planes sat at the bottom of the Coral Sea—with their pilots.

Yamamoto was frowning because Hara had failed in his mission to land troops at Port Moresby in New Guinea, the launching pad they needed to invade Australia. For the first time in this war, a forward thrust by a Japanese invasion fleet had been shunted aside.

Creases deepened in Yamamoto's forehead when he read the casualty reports. Japan had "won" the Battle of the Coral Sea, but the victory was bitter. The *Zuikaku* had lost four out of ten pilots, the *Shokaku* three out of ten.

Yamamoto ordered King Kong Hara to take his remaining ships and join the ships massing to attack Midway beginning on June 4. But he knew that Japan's 200-ship fleet would come to Midway without some of her finest pilots.

**MAY 12:** *Burma, seventy miles from India*

Vinegar Joe upped the pace of his party to sixteen miles a day going up a mountain, seventeen coming down. He feared they would be mired in the coming monsoon rains or cut off by pursuing Japanese.

The monsoon rains began to sweep over the party, drenching their clothes, turning mountain paths into slippery streams. The 114 men and women stumbled and fell, rose, fell again. But no one stopped, fearing a lash of curses from Vinegar Joe. The Chinese and Burmese nurses tried to cover over the general's tirades by singing Christian hymns.

**MAY 16:** *Washington, the War Department*

Houston newspaper publisher Ovetta Culp Hobby saluted the General. He returned the salute, then shook her hand. The occasion: a press conference to introduce Hobby as the first director of the new Women's Auxiliary Army Corps, America's first female soldiers.

Thirty-seven-year-old Major Hobby told reporters that WAACs would hold sixty-two non-combat jobs. A WAAC Officers Candidate School would soon be set up for volunteers, she said, "one for whites, another for Negroes."

Women could volunteer at Army recruiting stations. The age limits were twenty-one to forty-five, height from sixty to seventy-two inches, the weight "proportionate" from 114 to 171 pounds. She said WAACs could wear makeup "in moderation" and tint their nails "inconspicuously."

**MAY 19:** *The White House, a reception room*

The President was wheeled into the room, the familiar grin on his wide face, his cigarette holder stuck at a jaunty angle, and his right hand extended. "Welcome home, general!" he shouted as photographers' bulbs glittered.

Jimmy Doolittle, a lieutenant colonel when he entered the room, learned that one prediction had come true. He had come home—rescued and flown to India by the Chinese—to be promoted to brigadier general. A door opened and Mrs. Doolittle rushed into her husband's arms. She had been flown here from California and kept in hiding by Roosevelt, who loved to play tricks. A minute later a second prophecy came true. The President pinned the Congressional Medal of Honor, the nation's highest, on Doolittle's chest.

All of Doolittle's raiders had come home safely except three who were killed in crash landings and eight who had been captured by the Japanese.

Doolittle told General Marshall that he feared what the Japanese might do to those eight captured men.

**MAY 21:** *Imphal, India*

Vinegar Joe marched into the town, his 114 Burma survivors dragging behind him. The General came out of the jungle, wrote one reporter, "looking like the wrath of God and cursing like a fallen angel." He had lost twenty pounds off a skinny body that shook with fever, his skin yellow with jaundice. But, as he had promised them, he had taken out his people intact, not a man or woman lost in Burma. No British or Chinese general could say the same. Of some 25,000 British, Burmese, and Chinese soldiers who had tried to defend Burma against the Japanese invaders, one of every two was dead, wounded, or missing.

American reporters quizzed Stilwell on how the war was going in what was being called the China-Burma-India (CBI) Theater. Stilwell knew that Americans were reading newspaper stories trumpeting great victories over the Japanese in China. Reporters in Chungking believed Chiang Kai-shek propaganda claims. In America their stories were headlined: "Stilwell's China Troops Trap 50,000 Japs" and "Chinese Kill 20,000 Japs in Single Battle."

Stilwell wanted to warn America that it was losing in the CBI. "I claim we took a hell of a beating in Burma," he told the reporters. "We got run out of Burma and it was as humiliating as hell."

**MAY 21:** *San Francisco, California*
"For the first time in 81 years," the *Chronicle* proudly reported today, "not a single Japanese walks the street of San Francisco."

**MAY 21:** *Pearl Harbor, Hawaii*
Lieutenant Commander Joe Rochefort stared at the intercepted Japanese messages in the basement office of Hypo, the secret name for Pearl Harbor code breakers. American intelligence officers had broken codes of the Japanese army. They could read about half the messages that Yamamoto was sending out to his admirals at sea. And many of those messages mentioned the codewords AF as Japan's next target.

But what was AF? Back in Washington, Admiral Ernest King, the Navy's chief of staff, thought it was Hawaii. Rochefort's boss, Admiral Chester Nimitz, thought AF might be the American West Coast. But Joe Rochefort guessed it was Midway. He contacted a naval officer on Midway and told him to radio an uncoded message to Pearl reporting a drop in the island's fresh-water supply. Rochefort knew that the Japanese were eavesdropping on Midway's radio calls.

**MAY 22:** *Pearl Harbor, Hawaii*

Joe Rochefort slapped a hand gleefully across his desk. He had just intercepted a message from Admiral Yamamoto telling his admirals that AF was short of water.

Rochefort was now certain that AF was Midway. He ran to the office of Admiral Chester Nimitz, the craggy-faced, frosty-eyed commander of the Pacific Fleet.

Nimitz listened to Rochefort. Then he picked up a phone and ordered every seaworthy battleship, cruiser, carrier, and destroyer to gather at Pearl Harbor, take on ammunition, and sail to meet the Japanese off Midway on June 4. He knew it was a naval force mightier than any Yamamoto expected to face.

**MAY 27:** *On a road near Prague, Czechoslovakia*

Reinhard ("the Hangman") Heydrich, assistant chief of Hitler's Gestapo secret police, sat next to the driver as his car sped toward Prague. Two days earlier the pale, thin-lipped

Heydrich had watched the hanging of a hundred Czech and Polish resistance fighters. Standing in front of the gallows, he announced that the Gestapo had "crushed all resistance in Poland and Czechoslovakia."

The driver braked the car at a sharp hairpin turn. A man stepped toward the car and hurled a brown object that banged against the car's front fender.

The bomb's blast knocked the car on its side, its right wheels spinning in clouds of black smoke.

German soldiers pulled out the gasping Heydrich. Two hours later he writhed in pain while surgeons took out the bomb slivers that had cut his spine in two.

**MAY 28:** *Bir Hacheim in the Libyan desert*

Oberlieutenant Heinz Werner Schmidt felt a shiver go through him. Crouched in a low trench, he saw row after row of the British Eighth Army's new American-made tanks, the General Grants, roar toward him through the shimmer of the desert heat.

Schmidt ordered his biggest guns to start firing. The lead Grant stopped, spun by a direct hit. Flames burst from its turrets. But shells skidded off the other Grants. Cannons roaring, the Grants thundered at the German line.

Schmidt dropped to the bottom of the trench. The toes of a dead man's boots dangled in front of his eyes.

"The earth trembled," he later wrote. "My throat was like sandpaper. This, then, was the end. . . . My fiancée would be told, 'With deep regret we have to inform you that . . .' And what would it mean? That I was just a bloody mess in the sand at an unidentified spot at an unimportant point in the desert."

A tank crunched the dirt near the trench. Schmidt pulled a blanket over him, thinking that "a blanket is not much good against a bayonet."

He heard voices shouting in English. Prisoners were being rounded up. After about fifteen minutes he heard the tanks roar away.

He and a few other survivors waited until night, then trudged back to Rommel's headquarters. Oberlieutenant Schmidt had started this day with 350 men. He now commanded thirty.

**MAY 26:** *London, England, 10 Downing Street*

The Prime Minister puffed on a cigar as he read the latest reports from General Alan Ritchie, commander of the Eighth Army. Churchill sensed that Rommel was building up his Panzers for a stab at Tobruk and the fresh water he needed to take Egypt and the Suez Canal. "This may be the biggest encounter we have ever fought," Churchill cabled Ritchie. "But Tobruk must not fall."

## Chapter Six

**JUNE 4:** *Prague, Czechoslovakia*

Heinrich Himmler, chief of the Gestapo, announced that Reinhard Heydrich had died after four days of suffering. Himmler said that 100 Czechs would be hanged to avenge Heydrich's murder. Himmler added ominously that "the hiding place of the killers has been found."

**JUNE 4:** *From 5 A.M. to 3 P.M., in the Pacific about 200 miles from Midway Island; aboard the Japanese aircraft carrier* Agaki, 5:30 A.M.

Admiral Nagumo stood on the bridge of his flagship, leading a parade of 165 warships, including four heavy aircraft carriers. Just after dawn more than 100 torpedo-carrying bombers had taken off from the carriers and roared toward Midway. They would begin the three-day air and naval bombardment of the garrison, leaving the Americans dead or stunned in smoking rubble when 5,000 Japanese invaders came ashore on June 7.

Nagumo and his two air officers, Commanders Genda and Fuchida, watched the planes dwindle to dark specks in the morning sun. Six months earlier all three had stood on the deck of this carrier as it sent off planes that surprised the Americans sleeping at Pearl Harbor. The three told one another that the Americans would get a second surprise this morning. Fuchida told them in Japanese, "Once again we will mow the Americans down."

**JUNE 4:** *Pearl Harbor, Hawaii, 6:30 A.M.*

Nimitz grabbed the radio message from Midway. The garrison was being bombed by carrier planes. He glanced at his watch. It was almost exactly the time that Rochefort had predicted the Japanese would attack. Out there, as Hypo had learned, were four big Japanese carriers. Nimitz, outnumbered three to one, had hurriedly put together about fifty ships, hoping to find the Japanese carriers and sink them. If American bombers sank the carriers, the Japanese would not be able to provide air cover for their troops landing on Midway. American planes could bomb and strafe the troops as they came ashore.

Nimitz had told his two task force commanders, Rear Admirals Raymond Spruance and Jack Fletcher, to search for the carriers where Hypo had said they would be. As Japanese fighters and bombers zoomed low to attack Midway, Spruance and Fletcher sent off dozens of torpedo bombers and dive bombers from the *Hornet,* the *Enterprise,* and the *York-*

*town.* The stubby-winged planes hurtled toward the four Japanese carriers some 200 miles away.

**JUNE 4:** *Aboard the* Agaki, *8:30 A.M.*

Admiral Nagumo and Commander Genda watched their planes return from Midway. A scout pilot had just radioed to *Agaki* that he had sighted at least one American carrier circling Midway. Nagumo knew he had to knock out that carrier before his troops could go ashore. He had held in reserve more than 100 attack bombers. Should be bring them up from their below-deck hangars and launch them at the American carrier? Launching would take at least one hour. During launching, he would have to wave off his Midway bombers, who were short on fuel and would have to ditch in the sea and be lost. He decided to hold off the attack and bring in his bombers.

**JUNE 4:** *Aboard the U.S. carrier* Enterprise, *9:00 A.M.*

Admiral Spruance paced the bridge. He had sent out his planes almost two hours ago. Not one had yet reported sighting the Japanese carriers. On the bridge American nerves were stretching to breaking points.

**JUNE 4:** *Aboard the* Agaki, *9:10 A.M.*

Admiral Nagumo and Commander Genda talked to the bomber pilots returning from Midway. They had torn up the main is-

Navy torpedo bombers, named Avengers, fly in formation. Torpedo bombers tried to come in low over the water to launch their deadly "fish" at warships, but most of the American torpedo bombers in 1942 lumbered in so slowly that they were easily shot down by Japanese gunners. Winston Churchill wept openly when he was told how an entire squadron of American torpedo-bomber pilots was wiped out during the first hours of the Battle of Midway. (*Photo courtesy of the National Archives*)

land's runway and shot down twenty American fighters and bombers. But planes were still landing and taking off from Midway. Nagumo decided to order a second strike at Midway, once again postponing the attack on what he thought was only one American carrier.

Where were those bombers that had taken off from Midway? Genda asked himself. Then he saw them, a slow line of torpedo bombers lumbering toward the three carriers like "waterfowl flying over a lake," Genda thought to himself. The carrier's guns were roaring, small clouds of black smoke dotted around the clumsy bombers. The *Agaki* shot down eight and sent eight others fluttering away, too damaged to fight.

"This is fun," Genda said to himself. But, he wondered, where are the planes from that American carrier?

**JUNE 4:** *In a Devastator torpedo bomber from the* Hornet, *approaching* Agaki, *9:30 A.M.*

Ensign George Gay aimed the nose of his plane, his torpedo slung below him, straight at the pom-pom guns. Bullets from pursuing Japanese Zekes and Zeros pounded his plane. His tail gunner was already dead. Devastators were blowing apart all around him. A wing hurtled by his cockpit, narrowly missing him.

The twenty-one-year-old ensign let go his torpedo, then swerved upward, missing the *Agaki*'s bridge by ten feet. "I could see the little

Jap captain up there jumping up and down and raising hell.''

Gay soared over the bridge, trailed by five Zeros. Their bullets tore apart the Devastator's controls. The plane dived into the water.

The impact knocked Gay unconscious. The shock of cold water awakened him. He struggled to the surface, grasping his life jacket. He covered his head with a black cushion so the Japanese gunners would not see him, and floated amid the fury of the biggest air-sea battle ever fought up to now.

**JUNE 4:** *Aboard the* Hornet, *10:05 A.M.*

S pruance and his staff gathered near loudspeakers that broadcast the garbled, static-splintered radio messages from pilots to the ship and to one another. They heard voices shout, "Look out . . . he's going down. . . . Zekes behind you . . .''

All fifteen of the *Hornet*'s Devastators, Ensign Gay's among them, had been blasted out of the air. So far, thirty-four of forty-one American attack planes had been downed by Japanese guns. And not one American bomb or torpedo had touched a Japanese ship.

**JUNE 4:** *Aboard the* Agaki, *10:10 A.M.*

S tanding on the bridge, Commander Genda heard the gunners shouting from below as they winged shells at the attacking Americans. "Five planes left . . . three left . . . two left . . .

one left . . ." Then a final shrill scream: "All shot down!"

Shooting down the American planes "is a lot of fun," Genda said to Fuchida. But there had been so many of them! Genda now suspected there was more than one carrier throwing planes at them. And the Americans had *not* been surprised. It even seemed, he thought, as if the Americans had expected them. This was not the weak force that Yamamoto had counted on overcoming for an "easy and almost-certain Japanese victory."

Genda glanced down at his flight deck, crammed with cans of gasoline, bombs, torpedoes, and planes loaded with explosives. The decks of the other three carriers are also filled with planes being readied for a second strike at Midway. If an enemy bomb hit that deck . . .

Genda decided to tell Admiral Nagumo that they should waste no time in launching those planes—not at Midway but at those carriers out there somewhere.

**JUNE 4:** *20,000 feet above the Pacific, 10:25 A.M.*
Lieutenant Commander Wade McClusky had vaulted off the deck of the *Enterprise* two hours before, searching for the Japanese carriers with his two squadrons of Dauntless dive bombers. He spotted a destroyer and followed it.

He gasped at the sight. Spread out below him and glittering in the morning light were two Japanese aircraft carriers ringed by cruisers.

McClusky's twenty-four dive bombers banked and screamed downward at 350 miles an hour at the two carriers, the *Agaki* and the *Kaga,* each caught with their fighters sitting helplessly on their decks.

**JUNE 4:** *Aboard the* Agaki, *10:26 A.M.*

C ommander Fuchida heard a lookout shout: "Hell divers!" He looked up at the black-tipped noses of the dive bombers hurtling toward the decks of the *Agaki* and *Kaga,* both awash with gasoline. Knocking down all those American attack planes had taken too much time. Now there was no time to launch the carrier's planes, sitting like defenseless ducks on the flight deck.

**JUNE 4:** *5,000 feet above the Pacific, 10:27 A.M.*

F or an hour after leaving the *Yorktown,* Commander Maxwell Leslie's seventeen dive bombers had searched for Nagumo's armada. They spotted a column of smoke, veered westward and now looked down at the two other carriers, *Soryu* and *Hiryu,* directly below them.

**JUNE 4:** *Aboard the* Agaki, *10:30 A.M.*

T he first 1,000-pound bombs hit the deck so hard that 200 men were thrown over the side into the churning sea. Fuel tanks, bombs, and torpedoes exploded, balls of fire enveloping planes and screeching sailors.

An explosion knocked Genda onto his knees. Flames singed his shirt and pants. He rose groggily, saw Fuchida, and shook his head sadly. *"Simatta!"* ("We goofed!") Genda said.

Flames licked at the feet of Admiral Nagumo, who refused to budge from the bridge. He would go down with his ship, he said, rather than go home a disgrace after losing his ship. Two officers had to drag him from the flames to a waiting boat.

Gasping and choking amid smoke and flames, Genda and Fuchida went over the sides of the sinking *Agaki*. They floundered in the sea until plucked out by circling destroyers. From the deck of a destroyer, Genda and Fuchida watched fiery explosions rock the *Agaki*. They saw black smoke plume straight up into the sky from the *Kaga,* balls of orange fire belching from bow to stern. Fuchida and Genda turned their eyes away from the two sinking carriers.

**JUNE 4:** *Aboard the* Soryu, *10:40* A.M.

The carrier's skipper, Captain Ryusaku Yamagimoto, looked up helplessly as Commander Leslie's seventeen dive bombers streaked down in three waves. He had also been too busy fighting off American planes to send up his planes as umbrellas against an air attack. The bombs hit like sledgehammers among the bombs and torpedoes, planes exploding, pieces of steel, bone, human hair and flesh plastering the decks. Flames wrapped like red tongues around Captain Yamagimoto, who shouted the Japanese war cry, *"Banzai!"* before he vanished in a ball of fire.

Minutes later 1,000 *Soryu* officers and sailors thrashed in the water as their burning carrier plunged to the bottom.

**JUNE 4:** *Aboard the* Yorktown, *11:50 A.M.*

"The attack is coming in, sir," the radar operator told Admiral Fletcher. Radar had picked up forty aircraft closing in on the *Yorktown,* the planes launched by the *Hiryu,* which had scooted away when Leslie's dive bombers attacked the *Soryu.*

Crewmen scramble away from fires on the listing deck of the U.S. aircraft carrier *Yorktown* after she was hit by a torpedo from a Japanese submarine during the Battle of Midway. *Yorktown* had been badly damaged in the Battle of the Coral Sea a month earlier but repaired so quickly at Pearl Harbor that sailors called her return "a miracle" as she ploughed into her last fight. *(Photo courtesy of the National Archives)*

Fletcher sent up his Wildcat fighters to meet the Japanese Zeros that were escorting the dive bombers. Planes swirled, crossed, dived, and climbed in the sky high above the *Yorktown.* Sailors cheered whenever a plane with a red ball on its wings tumbled down to splash into the ocean.

The Japanese dive bombers skimmed across the waves trying to come in below the trajectory of the carrier's guns. One-hundred-pound shells whizzed from the guns, planes coming apart 100 yards away from the ship.

One plane came through the blizzard of shells. It dropped a bomb that left a gaping crater in the flight deck. A torpedo plane sent one of its "fish" deep into the *Yorktown*'s boiler room. Explosions shook the giant ship, and it shuddered and stopped. Fires swept close to the ship's magazines that were filled with explosives.

**JUNE 4:** *Aboard the* Enterprise, *3:00 P.M.*

A scout plane located the *Hiryo,* the fourth and last surviving Japanese carrier. Spruance ordered a launch of twenty-four bombers, keeping his fighters to protect his carrier.

The bombers caught up with the *Hiryo,* zoomed down through thick antiaircraft fire, and left the ship blazing. An hour later the *Hiryo* joined the Japanese navy's three other carriers—half its total carrier fleet—at the bottom of the Pacific.

**JUNE 4:** *Berlin, Harnack House*

Attending this conference were several generals and scientists, the meeting chaired by Albert Speer, the slim, hawk-faced chief of German war production.

A general told the conference that "Germany's one chance of winning the war would be by developing a weapon with totally new effects." He asked about nuclear power and if nuclear power could be used as a war weapon.

"Research into pure uranium 235," a scientist said, could produce "an explosion of quite unimaginable force."

He told Speer and the conference that "the Americans seem to be pursuing this research with particular urgency." He knew of scientists who had fled Germany, he said, who were now working in America on a project that related to uranium 235.

"How large an atomic bomb would be needed to destroy a city?" a general asked. At mention of the words "atomic bomb," generals and scientists—and Speer—looked up, their faces showing surprise and attention. None had ever heard of such a weapon.

"No larger than a pineapple," the scientist said, cupping his hand as if holding a small pineapple.

Speer jotted a note to remind himself to talk to Hitler about how Germany could begin work to build an atomic bomb.

**JUNE 5:** *Aboard the* Yamoto, *2:20 A.M.*

Admiral Yamamoto ordered Admiral Nagumo to flee toward Japan and get out of range of Spruance's bombers. The Hero of Pearl Harbor wondered how the Americans had known his fleet would hit Midway.

**JUNE 5:** *Aboard the* Enterprise

Ensign Gay climbed up the rope and swung his body onto the ship's deck. He had floated in the water for almost twenty-four hours until fished out by a seaplane that spotted him. Fellow pilots had given him up for dead. They shook his hand and listened to his eyewitness report of how they had sunk the *Agaki* and the *Kaga.*

**JUNE 7:** *150 miles off Midway*

Admiral Fletcher had taken his crew of 2,270 off the *Yorktown* while repair crews tried to fix her boilers. A Japanese submarine sneaked close to Waltzing Matilda, as her crew fondly called *Yorktown.* The sub winged two torpedoes into her side. As American warships stood by, their colors at half-mast, "she uttered a sighing sound," wrote Navy intelligence officer Charles Mercer, "and rolled over, her tumbling loose gear making a death rattle. Then she sank in two thousand fathoms."

She was the last casualty of what Mercer and others would call the Miracle of Midway. Outnumbered three to one in ships and fighting faster planes, the Navy and its flyers had sunk four carriers and a heavy cruiser, destroyed 322 planes, and killed more than 2,500 Japanese seamen and flyers. The American losses: one carrier, one destroyer, 307 dead, and 147 planes lost, most them obsolete planes like Gay's Devastator.

**JUNE 8:** *Pearl Harbor, Pacific Fleet headquarters*

Admiral Nimitz shook the hands of Commander Rochefort and his Hypo code breakers. More than 100 brave young pilots had lost their lives, but they had kept Nagumo too busy to launch his planes to destroy the American carriers. Yet the victory at Midway, Nimitz said, "was essentially a victory of the Navy intelligence men" like Rochefort. What Nagumo and Yamamoto did not know—that the Americans were prepared and waiting—had hurt them. Twice in one month a thrust forward by the Japanese naval tide—this one aimed at the American coast—had been turned back.

**JUNE 9:** *Lidice, Czechoslovakia*

A dozen German army motorcycles roared down the cobbled main street of this town of 1,200 people. Most of the men were coal miners and woodworkers.

Soldiers leaped off the motorcycles, rifles strapped to their backs. They banged on doors. They ordered men, women, and children to line up near the 500-year-old St. Martin's Church.

A Gestapo officer shouted through a bull-horn that the town of Lidice had hidden the killer of Reinhard Heydrich. "The people of Czechoslovakia must choose between collabo-rating with the Army of the Third Reich or death," he bellowed. "You have chosen death."

The soldiers marched all the men and teen-age boys out of the town. Wives and mothers watched white-faced as the men and boys— more than 400 — were led past the church. They vanished into the summer dusk.

Many of the women fell to their knees, praying to St. Martin. The roaring of machine guns erupted like summer thunder. The wom-en screamed, knowing their men were being slaughtered.

The guns barked for almost five minutes. Moments after the last sharp pistol shot, the Gestapo officer came back to the assembled women. He gestured to the soldiers, who wrenched small children from their mothers' arms and bundled them into trucks. The officer told the women that the children "are being moved to educational institutions."

Trucks roared away, carrying the wide-eyed, weeping children. The officer told the women and teenage girls that they would be sent to concentration camps.

As the women and girls climbed into trucks, German bulldozers smashed into the town's houses. Soldiers poured cans of gasoline to set houses ablaze. Flames leapt from the roof of 500-year-old St. Martin's. When people came to Lidice in the morning, they saw only a black scar across the green countryside. Lidice had been wiped off the map with one fiery stroke of the avenging German torch.

**JUNE 18:** *Hyde Park, New York*

Winston Churchill had landed in Washington in a Pan-American "Flying Boat" seaplane from England. A small plane flew him to the ancestral Roosevelt home perched high above the Hudson River. In a small sitting room overlooking the sun-speckled river, Churchill sipped a brandy, Roosevelt a cocktail.

Josef Stalin had been bellowing from Moscow that the French and British should cross the English Channel and invade France. That "second front" would make Hitler send troops from Russia, easing pressure on the Russian army.

Roosevelt told Churchill that General Marshall wanted to launch a second front by smashing across the channel and invading France. Churchill shook his head. He still dreaded a frontal assault that could end with the blood of British and American soldiers reddening the channel. The second front, he told Roosevelt, should be launched with an invasion of French North Africa. The troops would land in Morocco and Algeria, coming in behind Rommel's

Afrika Korps. Sandwiched between the Eighth Army and the invasion force, Rommel would be destroyed.

From Africa, Churchill argued, the British and Americans could strike across the Mediterranean to attack what he still called "Hitler's soft underbelly."

Roosevelt wanted a "face-to-face" battle against Hitler anywhere—so long as it took place soon, especially before the November 1942 elections. He told Churchill that he approved the North African invasion—codenamed Torch—later in 1942. What he didn't tell Churchill, however, was that he had told Marshall, and Marshall's chief war planner, General Dwight Eisenhower, to continue to plan for an invasion of France later in the year. Roosevelt was putting off making a decision between Roundup, the invasion of France, and Torch, the invasion of North Africa.

He did tell Churchill that the commander of the European Theater of Operations (ETO) would be the fifty-one-year-old Eisenhower, whom Churchill had just met. Churchill gave his agreement. "Yes," said Churchill of Ike, "although hitherto unknown, he is a remarkable man."

**JUNE 19:** *Tobruk, Libya, 7:00 A.M.*

Oberlieutenant Heinz Werner Schmidt peered through his binoculars as Stuka dive bombers came down out of the rising

morning sun with full-throated roars. To blast
his way into Fortress Tobruk, the Desert Fox
had a new trick: The Stukas dropped bombs
that blew up the mines. Then Mark IV tanks
roared around the craters toward Tobruk.

Perched high on the turret of his tank,
which he called the Mammoth, the grimy-
faced Rommel had addressed his officers just
before dawn. He told Schmidt and other officers how he would capture the prize that had
eluded him for eight months in 1941. Tobruk
was guarded by 20,000 South African troops on
its west side, by about 10,000 other troops on
its east side.

Schmidt and Rommel's German and Italian
commanders would drive their tanks through
the opened lanes of the mine fields and aim for
the Tobruk harbor. That would split the garrison. The Afrika Korps would then blast at the
split garrison from rear and front.

Schmidt mounted his tank. The Panzers followed engineers who blew up barbed-wire for-
tifications. At 3:00 P.M. Schmidt could see the
harbor as he blasted at fleeing Tobruk defenders, firing from trucks.

Schmidt's tanks rumbled by rows of captured trucks. He realized they were the vehicles
of the South Africans, who now faced Germans
and Italians from the rear and the front.

At sunset, over 100 Mark IV tanks stood
with their guns circling the 20,000 South Africans.

"[They] have a choice," Schmidt said to his officers. "They can attempt a breakout, which is impossible without trucks, or they can fight to the end."

**JUNE 21:** *Washington, the White House*

President Roosevelt and Winston Churchill were finishing breakfast with their aides when a colonel came into the room and gave Roosevelt a pink-tinted paper. Roosevelt read the slip, then slowly handed it across the table to Churchill.

The message was from London and it began: "Tobruk has surrendered and a total of 30,000 taken prisoner."

At the table sat Lord Moran, Churchill's personal physician. Moran had seen Churchill stare at dozens of messages like this one telling of defeats—from Dunkirk to Singapore—but never had he seen the Prime Minister look so beaten.

"What can we do to help?" Roosevelt said quickly. He turned to General Marshall. He told Marshall that the British had lost half their tanks at Tobruk.

General Marshall had just sent 100 huge Sherman tanks to General Patton's First Armored Corps. Patton was building that corps in the California desert to be the spearhead of the invasion of North Africa or the invasion of France.

A Detroit woman brings a horseshoe and other pieces of scrap metal to a rally where scrap is being collected. Girl Scouts and Boy Scouts tramped through neighborhoods, knocking on doors, to ask people to go through their attics and garages for old metal and rubber that could be turned into new guns and tanks. *(Photo courtesy of The Library of Congress)*

"Mr. President," the chief of staff said, "it is a terrible thing to take a weapon out of a soldier's hands. But if the British need is so great that they must have them, then they shall have the hundred—right away."

## Chapter Seven

**JULY 2:** *Brisbane, Australia, MacArthur's headquarters*

Broad-shouldered Prime Minister John Curtin faced General MacArthur and argued that the American and Australian army should dig a line of forts across the northern rim of Australia facing New Guinea. That "Brisbane Line," said the Australians, could hold off the Japanese invading Australia—an invasion that Curtin expected almost any day.

No, said MacArthur, clutching the corncob pipe he liked to puff as he pondered strategy. He said he would resign as supreme commander in Southeast Asia if the Australian generals stuck to their idea of a defensive line in Australia. "We must attack, attack, attack," he said.

Curtin knew that no United Nations troops had attacked the Japanese anywhere in this seven-month-old war. "Attack where?" Curtin asked.

**JULY 3:** *On the road to Stalingrad, near Rostov*

P rivate Benno Ziesser glanced one last time at his watch. At 6:00 A.M., just after dawn, they would leap from their trenches and go "over the top" into what was nearly always a murderous curtain of Russian bullets. Benno heard the order: "Fix bayonets!"

Ziesser and his comrades in the German Sixth Army had been making these charges since June, when Hitler went on the offense. During the spring Hitler had built up his army with fresh troops from Italy, Rumania, and Bulgaria. He had badgered his generals with orders to take Stalingrad and capture the oil of the Caucasus.

Ziesser crept forward, firing his carbine. "I suddenly saw a Russian right under my feet in his trench," Ziesser later wrote in the story of his life as a soldier. "He was only above ground from the waist up. The nose under the tin hat was as broad as a boxer's.

Teenagers at an Orange, Texas, high school are sworn into the school's Victory Corps. Among the duties of corps members were organizing war bond drives and volunteering as mothers' helpers or babysitters for housewives who were working in war plants. *(Photo courtesy of The Library of Congress)*

"With one spring I was on him. With a jerk the green helmet swung around to face me and I saw a bearded peasant face gape in real terror as I reached him."

Ziesser told himself not to stick the bayonet at the Russian's bony face. He told himself to jab the bayonet at the top button of the Russian's uniform.

"I stopped thinking and did not feel anymore either, only saw that button and thrust with all I could put behind it. The bayonet bored deep into the flesh. . . . I landed right on the Russian, who just folded up soft under me. . . .

"For some time I felt absolutely beaten. Then I tugged out my rifle with its bayonet streaming blood, scrambled like a lunatic out of that hole, away from the dying man."

Before long, Ziesser's platoon moved at a dogtrot down the road toward Rostov, 300 miles from Stalingrad.

**JULY 3:** *Near El Alamein, Egypt*

General Rommel's tank rumbled eastward through the billowing dust, the sun a flaming red ball dropping below the rim of the desert behind the Afrika Korps. Rommel stood in the turret of his tank and watched the streaks of British artillery flare across the sky in front of him. The Afrika Korps had swept from Tobruk into Egypt at better than fifty miles a day. Rommel now stood some 100 miles away from Cairo and the Suez Canal.

Detroit men, women, and children line up to register for food-rationing books in the spring of 1942. The books contained coupons that consumers handed over, along with cash, to buy sugar, coffee, and other scarce items. When a person in one of these long lines started to grumble, he or she was told: "Don't you know there's a war on?" *(Photo courtesy of The Library of Congress)*

The British Eighth Army had brought artillery to this railroad crossing in the desert. It hoped to stall Rommel here while huge new American tanks, which General Marshall had promised, were being unloaded from ships in Cairo.

**JULY 4:** *Chicago, Illinois, the Loop*

Holiday moviegoers lined up to see *Juke Girl* starring Ronald Reagan and Ann Sheridan—"Those *Kings Row* Lovers in Love Again!" screamed newspaper ads. In *Kings Row*, Ann Sheridan played the part of a small-town girl in love with Reagan, the town's playboy. In *Juke Girl* she was a dance-hall hostess who loves Reagan, a farm boy.

Like many of Hollywood's leading men—Clark Gable and Jimmy Stewart among them—Reagan had gone into military service. A lieutenant in the Air Corps, Reagan was stationed near Hollywood making training films.

Chicago movie theaters, like those in other midwestern and eastern cities, were packed for the Fourth of July holiday. Everyone had to stay close to home because few drivers had ration coupons allowing them enough gas to drive very far out of town.

**JULY 6:** *Wolf's Lair, Hitler's Russian headquarters in Eastern Germany*

"An atomic bomb, Speer?" Hitler said, a note in his gruff voice indicating he thought Speer had gone mad.

Speer was telling Hitler about his conference with scientists a few weeks earlier during which he had learned that such a bomb might be possible. It would be so devastating, Speer had learned, that one atomic bombing might win the war.

Speer could see, however, that Hitler could not imagine such a weapon. "The idea of such a bomb," Speer would later write, "obviously strained his intellectual capacity."

Could the bomb be built soon? Hitler asked.

No, Speer said. But he told Hitler that German scientists should be given money to work on an atomic bomb.

No, Hitler said. The scientists were now working on rocket-powered missiles. He wanted that work to be speeded up, not slowed by work on an atomic bomb.

Then, in a rare good mood, Hitler said, "You know, Speer, one day these scientists will uncover so many secrets of nature that they will set the universe afire. But we will certainly not live to see it happen."

**JULY 10:** *New York City, Pennsylvania Station*

Mothers and wives were saying good-bye to sons and husbands, many of the men already in Army and Navy uniforms. Amid both laughter and tears, Private Walter Schub was kissing his wife, Jean. "Now we're sure to win the war," he told her. As Walter waved good-bye, Jean joined about 100 other women who boarded trains carrying them to Fort Des Moines, Iowa, the Officers Candidate School for WAACs.

**JULY 17:** *Washington, the Navy Department*

An official confirmed that 395 ships along the Atlantic coast and off south Florida had been sunk since the year began. More than 5,000 sailors, merchant marine crews, and passengers had died, said a Navy official, though he would not give an exact toll. "That," he said, "would be giving aid and comfort to the enemy."

**JULY 17:** *London, The Admiralty*

Prime Minister Churchill stared at a huge map in the Royal Navy's War Room. Red dots indicated the sinkings of United Nations ships in the Atlantic and in the North Sea. Convoys of British and American ships wove through the North Sea, dodging the torpedoes of submarines and the bombs of Luftwaffe planes. The ships carried tanks and guns to Murmansk in North Russia.

"Let us face a frightening truth," Churchill wrote that night in his diary. "We are losing ships faster than United Kingdom and American shipyards can build them."

Crewmen of a Navy destroyer watch a depth bomb explode off their stern as they chase after German submarines dogging a convoy, which is stretched out on the horizon. When wreckage and a widening patch of oil spread on the surface, the Navy men figured they had sunk the sub. But sub commanders often released flotsam and a stream of oil to try to fool their attackers. *(Photo courtesy of the National Archives)*

**JULY 17:** *Over the coast of France*

The gleaming Spitfire, a big green shamrock painted on its fuselage, roared over the beach, its guns blazing at German cannons. The Spitfire's pilot, redheaded, twenty-one-year-old Wing Commander Brendan ("Paddy") Finucane, with thirty-two German planes shot down, led all R.A.F. aces.

Following Finucane over the beach, his wingman saw a hidden machine gun. Its bullets sprayed Finucane's radiator. "You've had it, sir," the wingman shouted over his radio.

Finucane looked at his temperature gauge and saw the needle swing wildly. His engine might blow up at any instant. "I shall have to get out of this," he radioed his wingman.

He wheeled the Spitfire toward the distant English coast. His wingman tailed him. Ten miles from the white cliffs of Dover, the Spitfire suddenly dipped toward the white-flecked channel. "This is it, chaps," Finucane radioed pilots listening back at the base. The Spitfire dived into the water and sank like a stone.

**JULY 21:** *Berlin*

A reporter for a newspaper in neutral Turkey walked the streets and scribbled these impressions that he mailed to his newspaper: "This is a city of armless, legless, eyeless war wounded. It is a city where you line up for food and only cabbage and potatoes are all you can get. Most everything, it is said, is going to the front in Russia. Even the beer is watery."

**JULY 24:** *Washington, the White House, the Oval Office*

President Roosevelt signed a bill passed by Congress that set up a women's Navy auxiliary. It would have 1,000 officers and 10,000 enlisted women. They would be called WAVES (Women Appointed for Various Emergency Services). WAVES, unlike WAACS, would not be sent overseas, an official said, nor would they be put on combat ships.

**JULY 27:** *Los Angeles, California*

Mrs. Zelma Hanson was sworn into the WAACS and sent to Fort Des Moines, Iowa. An hour earlier her son, Richard, was sworn into the Army and sent to Fort MacArthur in California.

**JULY 29:** *London, the War Ministry*

In an underground shelter, code breakers scanned the message. A Berlin general had sent it, ordering a large convoy of ships to leave from Naples, in south Italy, carrying big Mark III tanks and oil to Rommel. The English had a machine, called Ultra, that could read the German military codes. It decoded and gave the British nearly all the messages being sent by Hitler and his staff to generals and admirals.

**JULY 30:** *Malta*

An R.A.F. officer took the message from London. He picked up a phone at this British air and sea base in the Mediterranean Sea. "A big convoy is leaving from Naples tomorrow for Tobruk in Africa," he told a wing commander. "We can start bombing the ships as they leave Naples and blast them all the way across the pond to Tobruk."

The R.A.F. officer put down the phone. He wondered, as he often did, how those chaps in London always seemed to know when and where those convoys were crossing to Rommel.

## Chapter Eight

**AUG. 1:** *Wolf's Lair, Hitler's Russian headquarters in eastern Germany*

Hitler was laughing. The Russians, he had just been told, were retreating toward Stalingrad. Hitler could smell the oil of the Caucasus.

"Why do I have to war against second-rate armies?" he asked his chief of staff, General Franz Halder.

The Russians are finished, he told Halder. He would push through the Caucasus and invade the even richer oil fields of the Middle East. By next year he would be shaking hands with Japanese generals in India. He told Halder that soon the British and Americans will be "to the point of discussing peace terms."

**AUG. 2:** *El Alamein, Egypt*

Rommel paced angrily up and down the dirt floor of the tent. He held radio messages from Tobruk in his hand. Convoys of ships had sailed from Italy to Tobruk with fuel and tanks, but British bombers had sunk three of every four ships. Screaming curses, Rommel told an aide that "spies in Italy must be tipping off the R.A.F. whenever one of those convoys leave Naples."

He knew that the British had a new commander of the Eighth Army, General Bernard ("Monty") Montgomery. And Monty, he also knew, now had those huge American-made tanks. They fired shells that blew apart his Mark IV tanks, the terrors of the desert until now. Montgomery now had twice as many tanks as Rommel.

**AUG. 4:** *Moscow, the Kremlin*

Generalissimo Stalin now commanded more than eight million troops, both men and women (the women fired machine guns, treated the wounded on the battlefield, and fought in fighter planes). A short, stubby-figured man, Stalin stroked his mustache to show his anger as aides told him that the Germans had pushed to within sixty miles of Stalingrad.

"What's needed is revolver discipline," Stalin growled. Officers, he said, should use their revolvers to shoot soldiers who took one step backward. He dictated an order to be published in *Red Star,* the Army's newspaper.

"The Russian Army has no right to retreat any farther. No post must be abandoned while one man is alive. Die—but don't retreat! If a soldier retreats, he will be shot!"

Marines leap from their landing boat, an LCI (Landing Craft Infantry), as it nudges into the sand at Guadalcanal. This was the first amphibious—from sea to land—invasion by American forces in World War II, but it would soon be followed by many more in the Pacific. *(Photo courtesy of the National Archives)*

**AUG. 7:** *Aboard a troop transport off Guadalcanal Island in the Solomons near New Guinea*

M arine rifleman Bob Stiles could not believe his eyes when he looked from the deck as the dawn's first light spread over the sea. He had never seen anything like this back in the Bronx. Warships stretched across the horizon. "It looked like the whole U.S. Navy was supporting us," he later said. "It was a good feeling."

The Pacific Fleet commander, Admiral Chester Nimitz, had decided to invade Guadalcanal and other islands in the Solomon chain. From those islands the Navy could guard ships ferrying guns and troops from Hawaii to General MacArthur's army in Australia. And from bases like Guadalcanal, the Navy could bomb the big Japanese air and sea bases at Rabaul on the island of New Britain.

While Stiles watched, the armada's guns belched flame. Their din caused marines in the First Division to clap their hands over their ears. Stiles saw trees on the island pinwheel into the sky.

Stiles climbed down nets on the side of the ship and dropped into a steel-fronted assault boat. The boats circled to form the first wave of attackers. The boats tossed in the high waves. Seasick and nervous marines threw up. "Keep the pukers on one side of the boat," Stiles heard a sergeant say. But the bottom of the boat was a mess.

Minutes later Stiles's assault boat churned through the white surf, its steel hull grinding against the sand of the beach. Stiles jumped out and ran low toward a clump of trees, gripping his M-1 Garand rifle. "Thank God there weren't any Japs firing at us," he said later. "Some of the guys were so sick they didn't care if the Japs hit them or not."

Stiles moved warily through the jungle, eyeing treetops for snipers. He and his platoon followed a path that led to the island's landing strip. They found half-eaten, still-warm breakfast plates. An officer said that the naval bombardment had chased the Japanese deeper into the thick jungle.

At dusk Stiles "chowed down" for dinner around tents set up near the landing strip. The first American attempt to regain territory conquered by an enemy had been, the marines told one another, "a piece of cake."

**Aug. 8:** *Washington, District of Columbia jail*

The coroner arrived first, followed by a clergyman. Six prisoners were taken from their cells. A rubber mask, with slits for the eyes and mouth, was placed over each man's head. Then, one by one, they were taken to the electric chair.

The six men had been sent ashore two months earlier from German submarines. They carried explosives to blow up American war plants. All six were seen coming ashore on Long Island and Florida beaches.

A military court sentenced them to death as spies. Reporters watched as each man was strapped into the electric chair. The jail's lights suddenly dimmed, sparks flew, the body jolted upright, then sagged. America had executed its first spies since the Civil War.

**AUG. 12:** *Guadalcanal*

Colonel Frank Goettge led a patrol of twenty-five marines down the trail toward the village. Leading the patrol was a Japanese prisoner. The prisoner had told Goettge that a large band of Japanese troops had scurried to the village when the marines landed a week earlier. He told Goettge that the troops were starving and wanted to surrender.

The marines came into a clearing facing the village and stopped, looking for a white flag. The blast of machine gun bullets cut down Goettge and the prisoner, killing each instantly. The marines dived for the cover of the jungle. Snipers picked them off one by one. Three survivors raced to a nearby lagoon, plunged in, and swam for the sea. Bullets spattered around them. Out of rifle range, they turned to see flashing Japanese bayonets butchering wounded and dead marines.

That night the three survivors crept back into the marine camp at the landing strip and told their story. No one on the Canal, as the Marines now called the island, ever again talked about "a piece of cake."

"Up to now," wrote one marine, "the Marines on Guadalcanal and elsewhere . . . did not realize that when you fight the Japanese, you could not expect quarter. They gave none and expected none. The killing war had started."

**AUG. 12:** *Moscow, the Kremlin*

He was "visiting the ogre in his den," Churchill told an aide about his first meeting with Josef Stalin. Churchill had flown from Cairo to Moscow to give Stalin the bad

Marines on Guadalcanal read their daily "newspaper," a bulletin board labeled the Guadalcanal Gazette. While one marine points to the latest news of the war on a map, others were probably just as interested in the latest baseball scores. As the Gazette shows, the Dodgers won two games against Boston. In 1942 the Dodgers were in Brooklyn and the Braves in Boston. And Philadelphia had an American League team called the Athletics, since moved to Oakland, California. *(Photo courtesy of the National Archives)*

news face-to-face: there would be no second front in France in 1942.

Stalin glared, the broad face frowning angrily. "Why are you British afraid of the Germans?" he growled.

Churchill's pudgy face turned even pinker than usual. But he let the insult slide by. He said the British and Americans lacked enough ships to land all the troops needed to cross the English Channel and get a toehold in France.

But there would be a second front this year, Churchill said.

Stalin's eyes flickered with interest. Where? he asked.

About a quarter of a million British and American troops, Churchill said, would soon land on the coast of French North Africa.

When? Stalin quickly asked. Operation Torch would begin within ninety days, Churchill promised.

"May God help this enterprise to succeed," Stalin said solemnly.

Churchill hid his surprise. He had thought that Russia's Communists were not allowed to believe in God.

**AUG. 15:** *Dover cliffs over the English Channel*

M en, women, and children had heard the roaring—"like a huge waterfall," one said. They crowded the cliffs, staring upward into the dusk as waves of American and British planes droned toward France. Cheers rose as someone said he had counted more than 1,000 planes—the biggest one-day air attack in history.

**AUG. 15:** *Wolf's Lair, Hitler's Russian headquarters in eastern Germany*

"Communism must be deprived of its shrine—Stalingrad," Hitler growled at General Halder. They stared at maps showing two huge German armies. Both were moving much too slowly toward Stalingrad, Hitler snarled. He decided on a new strategy. Army Group A was swung away from Stalingrad to attack Rostov, south of Stalingrad.

Halder told Hitler he was wrong. Army Group A had been fighting the Russians on a 500-mile front. It would capture Stalingrad within a week or two, he said. But now Army Group A had to fight on a front almost 1,500 miles long. "It's impossible for them to do that!" Halder said.

Hitler waved off Halder's protest. "You are too nervous," he snapped, eyes flashing. "And so you are making me nervous."

Hitler now ate alone in a concrete blockhouse, surrounded by guards. He walked alone at night, his huge Alsatian dog at his side, the guards always nearby. He told Goebbels he worried that one of his own generals might try to assassinate him.

**AUG. 19:** *Dieppe, a French village on the English Channel*

Twenty-three-year-old Franklin Koons, an Iowa farmer a year ago but now a U.S. Ranger, waded ashore. He was one of about 6,000 troops, mostly Canadian Commando raiders, who were making this hit-and-run invasion of France.

Koons sprinted up the beach with three Ranger buddies. German machine guns chattered loudly, whistling slugs at raiders huddled on the sandy beach.

Crawling on hands and knees, Koons reached the top of the beach. He saw a stable and dived behind a wall. A bullet whizzed over his helmet. He thrust his rifle through a crack in the wall and squeezed the trigger. His was the first shot fired by an American on European soil in World War II.

Crouched in concrete blockhouses on the side of the cliff over the beach, the Germans mowed down the Canadians as they waded ashore. Koons saw piles of bodies strewn from the water's edge to the top of the beach.

The Canadians advanced into that "wall of fire," as one later put it. "It seemed like a suicide mission," he said, "but we kept on advancing."

The Canadians fought into Dieppe's center. They dodged from house to house, gunning down Germans perched on rooftops.

Near noon, four hours after landing, the

Canadians and the American Rangers, Koons among them, clambered back onto their landing barges. They pulled away from the shore, their boats piled high with moaning and screaming wounded. German fighters strafed and bombed the boats, their exploding bombs tossing up waves that overturned boats.

Corporal Koons floated back to England unharmed. But of the 6,000 raiders, more than 3,600 were killed, wounded, or captured. Also lost was a destroyer, thirty tanks, and more than 100 fighter planes.

In England, British generals called the raid a success because it had probed German defenses against a second-front landing. One Canadian officer read what the generals had said and told a reporter, "If that nightmare in hell was a success, God have mercy on us when we try the real thing."

**AUG. 19:** *Kokoda Trail, New Guinea*

The sweaty, grunting Japanese soldier swung his machete into the thick jungle vines. Sweat streamed down his face—the temperature was a humid 120 degrees. He swung the machete for only a few minutes, then collapsed, panting on the green slime of the trail. He had opened the trail no more than a yard wide and a yard deep. Another soldier took his place and began swinging the machete, cutting another yard deeper until he collapsed.

They led a line of 14,000 troops, commanded by General Tomitaro Horii. The troops had landed at Buna on New Guinea's north coast. Now they hacked their way southward 100 miles through thick jungle and across cloud-draped mountains toward Port Moresby.

The Japanese had tried to capture Port Moresby by sea and had been thrown back in the Battle of the Coral Sea. Now they would try to capture it by land, driving overland across mountains and through jungle. Horii guessed that the Americans would never dream the Japanese would come at Port Moresby through what he called "this green slime."

**AUG. 22:** *Washington, the War Department*

Lieutenant General Lewis Hershey, director of the draft, said that the Army had swallowed up all the healthy unmarried men between the ages of twenty-one and thirty-five.

Air Corps soldiers go through early-morning calisthenics at a base in Georgia. From these basic-training camps—boot camps in Navy terminology—recruits were sent to camps where they learned how to be tail gunners, mechanics, pilots, or bombardiers, among other specialties. For many young Americans who had lived through the Great Depression of the 1930s, serving in the Army and Navy meant getting three meals a day for the first time in their lives. *(Photo courtesy of The Library of Congress)*

"We will run out of single men in a few months and then we must turn to married men," he said. "This country has never had a war in which we drafted boys of 18 and 19 but we will have to draft them in this war." Eighteen- and nineteen-year-olds, he said, could volunteer for the Army and Air Corps, and men between the ages of eighteen and fifty could volunteer to join the Navy.

### AUG. 25: *Seattle, Washington*

B oeing Aircraft workers received an E award from General Harold ("Hap") Arnold, commander of the U.S. Air Corps. A year earlier the workers had been turning out one to two B-17 Flying Fortresses a week. Now they were rolling out five per week.

### AUG. 26: *San Francisco*

A new Warner Brothers musical opened, starring two blond singing and dancing stars—Betty Grable and Jane Wyman. Ads proclaimed that this movie "is something to sing about, laugh about . . . a perfect tonic for our times."

### AUG. 30: *Northampton, Massachusetts*

A sophomore at Smith College, Catherine Dugan, told a reporter what college women would be wearing in the fall on wartime campuses. "Sense is taking the place of nonsense. We are finding it practical to wear slacks,

jeans and long skirts this year. They fit the
work we have to do. Besides, what's the use of
getting dressed up if there are going to be no
men on the campuses?"

Two young women march off to a field near
Washington, D.C., to help plant crops. They are
wearing uniforms proposed for a Woman's Land
Army, which would plant and harvest crops that
were in short supply because of the war. In 1942,
it was often said, "everyone wants to be in uniform." *(Photo courtesy of The Library of Congress)*

# Chapter Nine

**SEPT. 1:** *Boston, Massachusetts*

The Glenn Miller Orchestra opened at a theater by playing one of its latest recordings, "I'll Be Home for Christmas." Some people wept when they heard the last lines of the song, the words of a soldier writing home to his family.

Near the end of the show, the leader of the nation's most popular band announced that the band soon would be no more. As fans groaned, Glenn Miller announced that he would soon be Captain Glenn Miller, U.S. Army Air Corps.

**SEPT. 1:** *El Alamein, Egypt, Rommel's headquarters*

Rommel stared at the map showing the British tanks and artillery ringing the El Alamein railroad station. Rommel traced a finger across the map. He stopped at Alam el Halfa Ridge. If he could take that ridge, he could pour cannon shells down onto the British tanks around El Alamein. He told a tank commander to scrape together fifty of the Korps' best tanks and charge straight ahead at Alam el Halfa Ridge.

**SEPT. 2:** *Guadalcanal*

A captured Japanese soldier told a marine why so few Japanese soldiers on the island had surrendered. "At home I am listed as dead. I know I can never return to Japan. If I returned they would know I surrendered and my family would be disgraced."

**SEPT. 3:** *London, General Eisenhower's European Theater of Operations (ETO) headquarters*

Colonel Harry Butcher awakened Eisenhower with a cable from General Marshall in Washington. "There'll be [orders to do] something impossible in it," Eisenhower grumbled.

Ike Eisenhower nearly always wore a sunny smile. He had learned how to get along with political leaders like Roosevelt and his army boss, General Marshall, by giving them what they wanted. But weeks of arguing with Winston Churchill and British generals had left him so angry, said an aide, "I see steam coming out of his ears after every meeting with Winnie."

Ike and Marshall had been planning a cross-channel invasion of France. Ike told his aides that it would be "the blackest day in history" if Russia's eight-million-man army was swallowed up by Hitler before the Americans and English launched a second front in France.

But Churchill still wanted that second front to be in North Africa. Finally Roosevelt gave in to Churchill. He ordered Marshall and Ike to plan an invasion of North Africa. Ike had been planning the cross-channel invasion since December. "Now I'm back to where I was last December," he told Butcher. And now he had only two months to plan for the invasion scheduled for early November.

Operation Torch—the invasion of North Africa—had political complications. French North Africa was manned by French soldiers who had sworn allegiance to the Vichy government in unoccupied France. Vichy did what Hitler told it to do. Almost certainly, Ike told Churchill, the Vichy government would tell its troops and battleships in North Africa to hurl the invaders back from the beaches and into the sea.

Churchill told Ike not to worry. The French troops, he said, would not fight the British and Americans.

If Churchill's guess is correct, Eisenhower wrote in his diary, "we may gain a tremendous

Free French soldiers dash across the Egyptian desert during a charge at El Alamein against the Afrika Korps. The Free French were recognized by Churchill and Roosevelt as the true French government in exile, based in London and headed by General Charles de Gaulle. (Photo courtesy of the National Archives)

advantage in this war; if the guess is wrong, it would be almost as certain that we will gain nothing and will lose a lot."

But he had no choice. He had to land 100,000 troops on foreign beaches, and he had only two months to prepare for it. He told an aide, "The time has passed for dilly-dallying."

**SEPT. 3:** *El Alamein, Egypt*

American Army Sergeants Al Broer and Jerry Petano had arrived here with the new General Grant tanks to show the British how to drive them and fire their cannons and machine guns. Broer and Petano crouched in their tank, peering through slitholes at the wave of Mark IV German tanks advancing toward the ridge.

Dust billowing behind them, the Panzer tanks came closer, looming as large as battleships in front of the widening eyes of the two Americans. Their fingers tightened around the triggers of their guns.

"Hold your fire!" The order from Lieutenant Allan Anderson crackled on the earphones of their radios.

Both men felt shivers ripple down their back. In soldier lingo, they were "firing their first shots in anger." They had to ask themselves if these were their last few seconds of life.

"Now!"

The Grant tanks pumped steel shells the size of manhole covers at the German tanks. The Mark IVs stopped, jagged holes in their flanks.

Fires flamed from turrets. Germans flew out of turrets, their bodies burning. Roaring sounds deafened Broer and Pitano as a shell shook the Grant. But the German shells were glancing off the rocklike American tanks.

**SEPT. 4:** *Privolnoye, North Caucasus, Russia*

German troops had swept through the town a month earlier, on their way to Stalingrad. They slaughtered 370 Jewish families—men, women, babies—who had been hidden on a farm near the town, burning the bodies. They left after promising to buy the wheat that soon would be harvested on the steep slopes above Privolnoye.

Women and children harvested the wheat, their only food for the coming winter. The men were gone to war. Mothers knew that Stalin had ordered the earth scorched in front of the invaders, not a stalk of wheat left for a hungry German soldier. Russian soldiers were ordered to kill civilians who harvested food for the Germans.

Eleven-year-old Misha Gorbachev labored next to his mother, a strong-willed woman who often told him, "One doesn't have to take the things of life as they are—there must always be a better way!"

Now she was showing him how to shake the faces of sunflowers, digging at the soil with the fingers for the fallen seeds, which were a substitute for bread.

Misha hoped the Russians would come back to recapture Privolnoye. Maybe his father, Sergei, would come back with them. But he worried: What would Communist Commissars do if they saw that his mother and the other women had not scorched the wheat fields? Misha, as his mother called Mikhail Gorbachev, told himself that he would protect his mother. After all, as his mother had told him, the Great Patriotic War was making lots of eleven-year-old boys as brave as men.

**SEPT. 4:** *Dallas, Texas*

This story was told often in Texas, but no one was really sure it had actually happened. A man got into a bus and began to brag loudly about how much money he was earning in a war plant. "I hope this war goes on forever," he said.

A woman slapped him with her right hand. "That's for my brother who was killed at Pearl Harbor," she said. Then she slapped him with her left hand. "And that's for my husband who was killed on Bataan."

**SEPT. 10:** *Kokoda Trail, New Guinea*

Scouts for General Horii's 14,000-man army hacked their way into a clearing. At least 1,000 had died so far, dropping from disease or exhaustion, sucked up and vanishing in the quicksand of marshes, drowning in raging streams. But the head of the column now stood only forty-four miles from Port Moresby, the base the Japanese needed in order to strike at Australia.

Australian infantrymen had landed at Port Moresby, climbed the bluffs above the city, and now were digging in along the Kokoda Trail about five miles away from Horii's advancing column.

**SEPT. 15:** *Brisbane, General MacArthur's headquarters*

S tumpy Brigadier General Pat Casey was reporting to MacArthur on his visit to the thick jungles and spiny mountains of New Guinea, where the Japanese were snaking their way along the Kokoda Trail toward Port Moresby. Casey said he couldn't understand how any human could live in New Guinea, never mind fight a war there.

Casey told of swarms of biting ants, deadly spiders, and giant rats that drained men of their blood as they slept. Australian soldiers were trying to push back the Japanese on the Kokoda Trail. Four out of five Diggers, as Australian riflemen called themselves, were sick with dysentery, yaws, ringworm, and dozens of other tropical sicknesses. At night the soldiers had to pull blood-sucking leeches from their bodies. The bites of buzzing mosquitoes often turned into hideous, pus-filled boils.

Puffing on his pipe and pacing up and down the room, MacArthur listened to Casey. Then

MacArthur turned to his aides and said in a low, trembling voice, "We'll defend Australia in New Guinea."

Casey stared, astonished, as MacArthur explained why he had decided to defend Australia in the mountainous jungles of New Guinea. The Japanese outnumbered him by at least two to one. If swarms of Japanese landed on the flat plains of Australia, they would race around him, cut up his army, then destroy it. But the thick jungles of New Guinea, he went on, would hamper the Japanese as much as they would hamper the Americans and Australians.

He looked around the room at the shocked faces of his staff. "You are surprised," he said, "and if you are surprised, so will be the Japanese."

**SEPT. 15:** *Aboard the U.S.* Wasp *off Guadalcanal*

Seaman First Class Kline Irwin had just come away from his battle station, manning a pom-pom gun. The carrier's crew had been at battle stations for most of the past twenty-four hours while the *Wasp* launched planes to attack Japanese ships rushing fresh troops to Guadalcanal. That morning a *Wasp* fighter had gunned down a Japanese bomber only a few miles from the *Wasp*. "The Japanese," Kline Irwin told a buddy, "know we are here."

**SEPT. 15:** *Aboard a Japanese sub a mile from the* Wasp

Turning the crank of the periscope, the commander watched the *Wasp* turn slowly into the wind as its planes took off from the flight deck. The commander ordered the firing of a "spread" of four torpedoes.

Moments later the torpedoes slithered one by one toward the turning *Wasp*.

**SEPT. 15:** *Aboard the* Wasp

The first explosion lifted Seaman Irwin out of his cot, and he crashed onto the steel deck. He heard yells: "We've been hit . . . torpedo . . . amidships."

The second and third hits rammed hard into the listing 22,000-ton *Wasp*. Irwin smelled smoke. Mobs of sailors were clambering up ladders. Irwin ran to a ladder and climbed two decks upward to the hangar deck, where the carrier's planes were stored.

He gaped at an inferno. Fires were igniting the fuel tanks of the planes. Hot machine guns popped bullets. The planes had been loaded with 500-pound bombs. The bombs were blowing up, metal fragments slicing into screaming sailors as they tried to throw the bombs over the side. Irwin saw a huge blue ball of flame, and then he was riding through the air. He crashed face down on the deck between two planes. Blood gushed from his nose and mouth.

He tried to sit up, too dazed to stand. Blue and yellow flames flared higher and higher all around him. The deck tilted sharply under him, the ship listing to its port side.

An officer stumbled over Irwin and told him the skipper had ordered all hands to abandon ship. Irwin tried to stand up but collapsed. The officer picked him up and threw him into the water some fifty feet below.

The shock of the sea water cleared Irwin's head. He swam to a floating mattress and clutched it. He felt something bump against his leg. He looked down and saw the yawning mouth of a shark.

"Sharks!" Men screamed all around him. Huge pools of flaming oil now dotted the water around the swimming sailors. The oil and flowing blood blinded Irwin, but he thrashed his legs wildly, trying to scare off the sharks.

Irwin heard a distant roar. Then something hard hit him in the belly, and he doubled up in the water, retching. Destroyers were dropping depth bombs. The explosions sent underwater shock waves that turned some of the wounded upside down.

Irwin had drifted a half mile from the *Wasp,* its flight deck now a huge cloud of black smoke and orange, yellow, and blue fires. He saw hundreds of tiny black dots in the midst of choking oil fires, the *Wasp*'s survivors waving frantically at destroyers coming to rescue them.

**SEPT. 16:** *Pearl Harbor, Pacific Fleet headquarters*

Admiral Nimitz stared grimly at the casualty reports. Of the 2,247 men on the *Wasp,* 193 had died, including 72 of the ship's

79 black mess stewards. The first torpedo had exploded below their quarters. More than 350 *Wasp* survivors were wounded but, like Irwin, had been plucked from the water and most would live. The Pacific Fleet had lost the carriers *Lexington, Yorktown,* and now the *Wasp.* Nimitz had only two aircraft carriers—the *Hornet* and the *Enterprise*—to attack the Japanese ships that were at this moment rushing fresh troops to Guadalcanal to hurl the marines into the sea.

**SEPT. 20:** *Kokoda Trail, New Guinea*

The survivors of General Horii's force stared through their binoculars at the smoke rising from chimneys in Port Moresby, now ten miles away. General Horii had landed 14,000 men at Buna on New Guinea's north coast a month ago. Now he had fewer than 6,000, the rest killed by disease, drownings, exhaustion, snakes, falls from mountain peaks, or slugs from Australian riflemen.

Horii had no more rice to feed his emaciated troops. Japanese pilots told him by radio that thousands of American and Australian troops were landing in Port Moresby. Horii's sunken-cheeked face showed his surprise. He had been sure that MacArthur would bunch up his army on Australian beaches to hurl back an invasion.

Imperial Army Headquarters in Tokyo cabled Horii that he could expect no fresh troops to attack Port Moresby. Japan had to send fresh troops to Guadalcanal. It was now more important, Horii was told, to retake Guadalcanal. Then the Japanese could drive to Port Moresby and Australia.

Horii told his exhausted soldiers to turn their backs on the goal that had cost them so much. They would have to fight their way back to Buna through the torture-filled "green slime" in the mountains and jungles of New Guinea. Horii informed his soldiers they would fight on the beaches at Buna to hold the Japanese beachhead in New Guinea.

"No pen or words," he told his soldiers, could tell of "the magnitude of the hardships [you have] suffered."

**SEPT. 20:** *Washington, Office of Price Administration (OPA)*

More than 150 million new ration books were being printed, one for each American man, woman, and child, the OPA announced. War Ration Book No. 2, it said, would be distributed by Christmas. Like War Ration Book No. 1, which had coupons to buy a pound of sugar every two weeks, the new book would have coupons for meat, gas, rubber, or whatever else might be rationed "for the duration."

**SEPT. 22:** *Stalingrad, Vilny Street*

Soldier-correspondent Joachim Strieber dove to the ground as rifle bullets spattered against the wall of the building behind him. He looked up at the roof and saw three Russians firing at his squad of infantrymen. In this street-by-street, building-by-building fight for the city, he would report, "these Russian workers and soldiers suddenly vanish, seeming to run away, and then they reappear and suddenly we are surrounded."

**SEPT. 24:** *Wolf's Lair, Hitler's Russian headquarters in eastern Germany*

General Franz Halder saw Hitler begin to foam at the mouth as he listened to an officer's report. Halder, Hitler's chief of staff, knew that Hitler hated to hear bad news. The officer was reporting that German intelligence showed Stalin was mustering more than a million fresh troops to throw at the Germans attacking Stalingrad.

Fists clenched, Hitler ordered the officer to stop reading "any more of that idiotic twaddle."

Hitler had fired a number of top generals because he was angry they had not yet captured Stalingrad. Now he turned on the stocky Halder. "You and I have been suffering from nerves," he snapped. "Half of my nervous exhaustion is due to you. It is not worth it to go on." He told Halder he was fired. Hitler had become his own commanding general and chief of staff. Now no one could tell him what to do.

Hitler issued an order to General Friedrich Paulus, commander of the Sixth Army attacking Stalingrad. One of Paulus's commanders

Camouflaged in a white uniform on a snow-covered Russian field, a German soldier uses binoculars *(left)* to spot a Russian position. He shouts *(below)* the distance of the position to a mortar-firing unit nearby. The mortar crew *(right)* crouch in their hole, covering their ears to protect against the deafening blast, as one drops a shell into the barrel of the mortar, a small cannon used for dropping shells a short distance at a steep angle. *(Photo courtesy of the National Archives)*

had reported losing 1,000 men in a single day
as the Russians poured shells into the Germans
bunched up along the Volga River in front of
Stalingrad. The commander wanted to retreat
to where his men would be shielded from the
murderous Russian fire.

Hitler wanted no talk about retreat. "Where
the German soldier sets foot," he told General
Paulus, "there he remains!"

**SEPT. 26:** *St. Louis, Missouri, Sportsman's Park*

The Yankees' Ernie Bonham threw the first pitch of the first wartime World Series since 1918. More than 34,000 people, at least one in five in uniform, filled every seat. This was the first World Series broadcast overseas: men and women soldiers crouched over short-wave radios in England, Australia, and Africa. The Yankees had won five of the past six World Series, and most of their stars—sluggers Joe DiMaggio, Bill Dickey, and Charlie Keller—were still with the Bronx Bombers. The world champion Yankees were heavily favored over a St. Louis Cardinal team that had a bunch of young players—Stan Musial, Enos "Country" Slaughter, Mort and Walker Cooper—in the lineup. The Yankees won the first game, 7–4.

**SEPT. 27:** *Stalingrad, General Vasili Chuikov's command post*

Thirty corpses were strewn around the top floor of the warehouse. Shells from German artillery and bombs from low-flying planes shook the ramshackle building. Bowls of soup, put on a table an hour earlier, were now filled with bomb fragments.

German tanks rumbled through most of the city. General Chuikov's Sixty-second Army held a strip of land a few hundred yards wide along the docks of the Volga River. His soldiers and rifle-carrying factory workers huddled in three clumps of scattered factory buildings, the

Tractor Factory, the Barrikady Factory, the Red October Factory.

General Chuikov picked up a ringing phone as a shell's fragments tore holes in the wall above his head. Calling from Moscow was a Communist Party chieftain, the bearlike Nikita Khrushchev.

"What is your major need at the moment?" Khrushchev asked the General. Khrushchev feared the General would say he would have to surrender the city. If the Germans held Stalingrad, they would cut off Russia from its richest oil fields.

"More ammunition," Chuikov growled.

"You will get it," Khrushchev promised. He now knew that Stalingrad had the right man defending it.

# Chapter Ten

**Oct. 2:** *Kokoda Trail, New Guinea*

General Horii lashed out with his sword. The blade cut deep into the arm of a Japanese soldier, who reeled back, then collapsed in a bloody heap. A dozen other soldiers trampled over his body, surging past the General's flailing sword. They vanished down a steep mountain trail.

The Japanese retreat to Buna had become a mob's panic-stricken rush to survive. The hungry, diseased, bloodied troops wanted out of this hellish jungle that had killed more than half of them in little more than a month. Not even a general could stop a wild-eyed race to food and shelter at Buna.

Australian Diggers pursued the Japanese. Near a deep, fast-flowing river, the Australians cut off a band of Japanese troops, General Horii among them. Horii jumped on a horse and tried to escape across the river. In the middle of the foaming water, he fell off the horse, thrashed helplessly for a few moments, then was sucked under. The Australians found his body an hour later.

### Oct. 3: *Guadalcanal*

Resting in a rain-spattered tent, Lieutenant Richard Amerine, a Marine Corps fighter pilot, told how he had survived a week in the jungle behind the Japanese lines.

His plane had crashed into the sea off Guadalcanal. The twenty-two-year-old pilot swam three miles to shore, where he collapsed. He awoke to see a dozen Japanese only 100 yards away. He knew how they tortured prisoners, gouging out eyes, bayoneting and mutilating.

He crept into the jungle. His clothes were tattered; he had no shoes. He saw a Japanese soldier asleep. "I picked up a rock as big as my chest and bashed in his head with one blow. I had to have his shoes if I was going to live in this jungle."

He crawled close to a native village, hoping to steal food. A dog trotted toward him, sniffing. "I was hungry enough to eat anything by now," he said, "but the dog got away."

Japanese riflemen saw him, and twice he crashed into the thick jungle as bullets spattered around him. For the next five days he skirted Japanese outposts, sniffing for their garbage heaps. Discarded coconut shells saved him from starving to death.

One night he tried to slip by a Japanese outpost but was seen by a sentry. Amerine waved, pretending to be a Japanese soldier. The sentry began to follow Amerine, who tried to walk as casually as he could.

"I figured he was about five yards behind me. I whirled and shot him in the chest with my pistol. The explosion knocked him over backward."

Japanese poured out of tents, chasing after Amerine. He ducked under a log as Japanese boots flew over him. The Japanese could not find him in the jungle blackness. But after an hour, two soldiers sat down on the log and began to talk.

"They sat talking until dawn. I knew I had to get away from them by sunup or they'd surely see me. I rose up quickly and with one roundhouse swing I clipped both Japs with the butt of my pistol. One stayed down, but the other tried to get up. I hit him again and I could feel his skull cave in.

"That was the sixth day and I was in pretty bad shape. The coral had torn my Japanese shoes to shreds. I was just about famished and was bitten all over my body by insects."

On the seventh day he stumbled into a marine patrol. "Those marines," he said, "were the best sight I ever hope to see."

**Oct. 3:** *Tokyo, the Imperial Palace*

Premier Hideki Tojo arrived to confer with Koich Kido, the Emperor's secretary. Tojo told Kido that the eight American flyers captured after the Doolittle raid had been sentenced to death for machine-gunning civilians. The eight had denied gunning down anyone. Tojo asked that the sentences be commuted to life imprisonment.

Kido brought the request to the Emperor. He came back to tell Tojo that the Emperor would spare five of the flyers, but three, who had been accused of machine-gunning children, the Emperor said, must die.

**OCT. 6:** *New York City, Yankee Stadium*

At the plate stood the tow-headed, twenty-one-year-old rookie Whitey Kurowski. His St. Louis Cardinal team led in the World Series, three games to one. In this fifth game, the score was tied 2–2 in the top of the ninth inning.

As more than 60,000 fans roared and millions listened intently on their radios, Yankee pitcher Red Ruffing looked at the runner on first base, then threw to Kurowski. The rookie swung. The ball shot on a rising line toward the left-field seats. Yankee left fielder Charlie Keller leaped, but the ball soared over his glove and dropped into the seats.

That homer won the game, 4–2, and the World Series, four games to one, for the Cardinals. In the clubhouse after the game, players said good-bye, knowing that most would be in the Army or Navy the next season and would not see one another "for the duration."

**OCT. 10:** *Stalingrad*

Russian correspondent Konstatine Simonoff crept forward in the concrete shelter to get a better view of the fighting below him. Flames roared from shattered buildings all around him.

Talking later by phone to Moscow, Simonoff told an editor that Stalingrad "has no more inhabitants—only civilian and soldier defenders. The aged and the young have fled to caves above the city. They throw up wooden planks to defend themselves against the wind, the falling snow, the cold and the shells that whistle across the cherry-red sky for 24 hours a day."

"We were repairing tanks when the Germans broke into our factory," one gun-carrying worker had told Simonoff. "Our workers leaped into the tanks. We drove them straight at the Germans and chased them out through the gates."

An hour later Simonoff stood in a deep ravine along the Volga. A police chief and a university professor commanded workers guarding a road into the strip of land still held by the Russians. The two men shouted orders to women who stumbled as they hauled heavy loads of ammunition to machine gunners.

"German motorcycles coming!" the police chief shouted.

Simonoff heard the sputtering roars, then saw some twenty German motorcycle troops bouncing down the ravine. Hidden machine guns met them with a wall of slugs big enough to tear holes in tanks. German bodies flew off the motorcycles, some sawed in two, their motorcycles spinning crazily down the banks of the ravine.

Surviving Germans scrambled up the steep slope. Tommy gunners jumped from bushes, spraying bullets at their backs. Forty seconds after the attack, the roaring of gunfire stopped, bodies strewn over the ravine. An occasional pistol shot broke the silence as the Russians finished off the wounded.

"Stalingrad has taught us something," the professor told Simonoff. "It has taught us how to be merciless."

Oct. 14: *Shanghai, China*

The three American airmen who had bombed Japan were led by guards into the office of the warden, Sergeant Sotojiro Tasuta. The faces of all three were gaunt, bearded, and dirty after months of beatings, hunger, and solitary confinement in cramped, filthy cells. The oldest, twenty-eight-year-old Dena Hallmark, had to be carried on a stretcher. The warden told Hallmark and the other two Doolittle airmen, twenty-three-year-old Bill Farrow and twenty-one-year-old Harold Spatz, that they would be shot the next day. He said they could write brief letters to their families.

That night Dena Hallmark wrote to his mother: "Try to stand up under this and pray." Bill Farrow wrote to his father, "I'll see you all again in the hereafter." Harold Spatz wrote to his mother, "I died fighting for my country like a soldier."

### Oct. 15: *Shanghai*

The three American prisoners stood in a truck that drove them to a cemetery. Guards led them down a grass-lined path to where three white crosses had been stuck into the ground. A line of Japanese soldiers, clutching rifles, faced the crosses.

Sergeant Tasuta ordered the three Americans to kneel down facing the firing squad. Their arms were roped to the horizontal bars of the crosses. A soldier drew black *X*s across their foreheads as targets for the riflemen, then stood back.

The Sergeant shouted the order to fire. The one volley killed all three. The bodies were buried under the white crosses.

A Navy blimp floats over a convoy of cargo ships churning toward an East Coast port in 1942. The blimps spotted German U-boats. By putting naval gun crews on cargo ships and by convoying the cargo ships and tankers with destroyers, the Navy began to cut down on the number of ships torpedoed along the coast by German submarines. *(Photo courtesy of the National Archives)*

**OCT. 19:** *Washington, U.S. Maritime Commission*

Admiral Emory S. Land told reporters that seven more cargo ships had been sunk along the East Coast in the past week. That raised the toll to 508 ships sunk off the coast since December 7, 1941. The ships had carried 2,343 merchant seamen

Soldiers chat with young women at a United Service Organization (USO) social center. These USO centers were places for soldiers, sailors, or marines to mingle with young women volunteers at dances and small parties. From the point of view of the GIs, the only problem with a USO was one that is shown here: There were far more men than women. The young woman at left is wearing the shoes and socks worn by most "bobby-soxers" of the time. *(Photo courtesy of The Library of Congress)*

and passengers to their death, but fewer ships had been sunk in August and September, he said, "than during any month since February. We have not yet won the Battle of the Atlantic," Land continued, "but no longer is the German winning that battle. And we are now turning out more cargo ships than Hitler can sink."

**OCT. 20:** *New York City*

Manhattan's most elegant restaurants, such as 21 and the Stork Club, posted signs announcing that no meat would be served on Meatless Tuesdays. And signs on fast food places read, "Sorry, no hamburgers. Tuesday, you know."

**OCT. 22:** *Washington, the White House*

President Roosevelt ordered that the annual Army-Navy football game be played at Annapolis, site of the Naval Academy, instead of in Philadelphia, where it was usually played. Fewer people could attend the game at Annapolis, which would mean fewer civilians trying to get on trains packed with soldiers and sailors going to their posts. Posters in train stations now asked travelers: "Is This Trip Necessary?"

**OCT. 22:** *London, ETO headquarters*

General Eisenhower called in his top staff officers to review the plan for the Torch landings in North Africa, now set for the morning of November 8. A Western task force of some 200 ships and 35,000 troops would come in from the Atlantic Ocean to attack Casablanca, the capital of French Morocco. That task force was commanded by one of Ike's best friends, Major General George Patton. Ike worried that the small landing boats might be tossed over and troops drowned as they came ashore in the pounding Atlantic surf.

A Central Task Force from England with about 30,000 British and American soldiers would come ashore from the Mediterranean, landing near Oran in French-ruled Algeria.

An Eastern Task Force of about 35,000 British, Canadian, and American troops would sail from England and Northern Ireland and come ashore at Algiers in French-owned Algeria.

As Ike reviewed the plans, he worried: Would the 100,000 French soldiers in French

North Africa stay loyal to the Vichy government? Vichy was certain to order those troops to fight back against the invaders.

Roosevelt and Churchill helped spirit a French general, Henri Giraud, out of France by submarine. The French troops in North Africa respected Giraud as a fighting general who had been jailed by the Nazis. Churchill and Roosevelt decided to set up Henri Giraud and a French admiral, Jean Darlan, as the new leaders of French North Africa. They hoped Darlan and Giraud could persuade French troops to step aside while the British and Americans landed, perhaps without a shot being fired.

**OCT. 26:** *Chicago, Illinois, Hurley Machine Company*

Women workers at this ordnance factory turning out ammunition formed the WOWs (Women Ordnance Workers). They wore two-piece khaki uniforms with overseas caps. "Everybody," said a company official, "wants to wear a uniform."

**OCT. 26:** *Aboard the superbattleship* Yamato, *anchored at Truk in the Caroline Islands*

Admiral Yamamoto was still the Hero of Pearl Harbor despite the disaster at Midway. He had convinced Japan's military chiefs that Guadalcanal and the other Japanese bases in the Solomon Islands had to be held.

Both sides were rushing warships to Guadalcanal to guard ships bringing in fresh troops and supplies. Now, argued Yamamoto, was the time for the huge Japanese force—four carriers, five battleships, fourteen cruisers, and fifty-five destroyers—to annihilate the American Pacific Fleet more than 2,000 miles from its base at Pearl Harbor.

OCT. 26: *Nouméa Island in the Solomons*

A PBY scout plane had spotted the Japanese task force massed near Guadalcanal. The pilot reported it to the new commander of the Navy's Southwest Pacific Fleet, the bulldoglike Admiral William Halsey, who knew that his boss at Pearl Harbor, Admiral Chester Nimitz, wanted the Navy to stop taking Japanese blows and start handing them out.

The marines on Guadalcanal had thrown back fierce charges by the Japanese at Henderson Field, Guadalcanal's landing strip. Both sides wanted Henderson for launching land-based planes to attack enemy ships bringing in troops to the island. Halsey's fleet had only two carriers, the *Hornet* and the *Enterprise*. But as long as the marines held on to Henderson, Halsey could send land-based planes at the Japanese carriers and battleships off Guadalcanal.

Halsey decided he had to attack while the marines still held Henderson Field. Just before dawn he sent out the order to his task force: "Attack—repeat—Attack!"

**OCT. 26:** *Aboard the* Hornet *near Guadalcanal, about 9:30 A.M.*

"The best way to win a carrier-against-carrier battle," naval officer Samuel Eliot Morison later wrote, "is to bomb the other fellow's flight decks before he can launch a strike. The next best method is to knock down his planes" before they get to you. "But if his strike gets through, the chances of escaping damage are slim."

The Japanese planes were now trying to get through to hit the *Hornet* before the American carriers could hit their four carriers. The *Hornet*'s crew stared up at the sky, filled with Zekes and Zeros battling American Wildcats.

Hundreds of black puffs dotted the sunny sky, ack-ack shells exploding around Japanese bombers. One Japanese "Val" dive bomber streaked through the puffs. Its bomb shattered on the *Hornet*'s deck. Hunks of jagged metal tore into American bodies, oil on the flight deck turning crimson.

A wounded Japanese plane wobbled toward the *Hornet*'s stack, bounced off it, and shattered. Its two bombs exploded, killing instantly a wave of Americans who had rushed toward it with fire-fighting gear.

Another torpedo bomber winged in low at deck level and stuck its torpedo in the *Hornet*'s midsection. The big carrier shivered and came to a stop, engines silent. Flames leaped across the flight deck. The *Hornet* sat like a bull's-eye for the next wave of attacking planes.

**OCT. 26:** *5,000 feet above the Pacific, about 9:40 A.M.*

The *Hornet*'s dive bombers saw the aircraft carrier *Shokaku* below them, its guns sending up flak that ripped holes in wings and fuselages. Lieutenant Jim Vose pointed his dive bomber straight down at the carrier, two Zekes hanging on his tail. Behind him, wind tearing at cockpits, screeched ten more *Hornet* dive bombers. They leveled at 500 feet and came in under the trajectory of the ship's flashing guns. Three 1,000-pound bombs cracked open the flight deck. The bombers swerved through clouds of black smoke as they climbed upward. Gunners shot at the pursuing Zekes. The carrier's flanks belched fire as it swung west toward Japan, out of this battle for good, out of the war for months.

**OCT. 26:** *Aboard the* Hornet, *about 3:15 P.M.*

Most of the fires had been quenched and a heavy cruiser was towing the *Hornet* when the dive bombers roared out of the sun to strike again. One torpedo blew up in the middle of the carrier. Balls of sickly green flame swept through the innards of the ship, and her huge hull listed sharply to port. Her captain ordered abandon ship. The 108 wounded were lifted off in baskets to circling destroyers; then her crew and skipper followed, leaving behind with the *Hornet* her 111 dead.

As one crewman scrambled down the side, he asked another, "Are you going to reenlist?"

"Yep, and on the new *Hornet!*"

**OCT. 26:** *In the Pacific off Guadalcanal, 10:45 P.M.*

Approaching Japanese battleships could see the *Hornet*'s funeral pyre from twenty miles away lighting up the night sky. American torpedoes had not finished her. An American destroyer fired a last shot, then scurried off as the Japanese battleships loomed closer. A Japanese destroyer rammed four torpedoes into the flaming hulk. Her crew shouted *"Banzai!"* — the Japanese shout of victory — as the ship that had brought the first enemy bombs to Japan vanished under 2,000 feet of water.

**OCT. 27:** *Pearl Harbor, Hawaii, Pacific Fleet headquarters*

Admiral Nimitz counted his losses. The *Hornet* and three destroyers had been sunk, the *Enterprise* damaged but still able to fight. The *Enterprise* was now America's lone carrier in the Pacific. The Japanese had three. The Japanese had lost one carrier temporarily and at least 100 of their best naval pilots forever.

**OCT. 28:** *Munich, Germany*

German mothers and fathers paid newspapers to print small notices about the deaths of their sons on the Russian front. This one was typical: "Our only son, Hurst Milleville, died as a hero during the heavy fighting. He went straight from the classroom to the front without our ever seeing him in uniform. His death has plunged us into unspeakable grief. He would have been 18 on November 1st."

# Chapter Eleven

**Nov. 1:** *Near Henderson Field, Guadalcanal*

Marine Private Barney Ross's company were the "point men," head scouts of a column assigned to push the Japanese away from Henderson Field. It was the island's only landing strip. Planes came into Henderson with supplies for the marines. The Japanese had to sneak in ships, but American warships were blowing one of two out of the water. Now thirty-three, the New York-born Barney had once been the welterweight boxing champion of the world.

He saw waves of Japanese soldiers coming down jungle trails toward them. The Japanese saw the marine point men. They sprayed Barney and his men with machine gun fire. Slugs whizzed off Ross's steel helmet. Two men dropped near him, one hit in the stomach, another in the leg.

Crawling under a stream of bullets, Ross dragged both men into a shell crater. Mortar shells burst all around him, dirt raining down on Ross and his two moaning buddies. Ross could have crawled back to his column through the mortar smoke, but he knew the two wounded men would be slaughtered by the Japanese.

Night came. Ross crept behind a log and began to pitch grenades at the machine gunners. They blazed back, and by morning Ross counted thirty furrows across his helmet.

Near dawn he had no ammunition left. He fixed bayonets to his rifle and the rifles of the two wounded men. "We were all scared to death," Barney said later. "All we could do was pray—and we prayed."

When light came, American artillery began to lob shells at the Japanese machine guns. Amid smoke and explosions that staggered him, Ross dragged the two wounded men back through the jungle. An officer said he would receive the Distinguished Service medal. "Tell 'em to give it to my company," Barney said. "This is no one-man show."

**Nov. 2:** *The desert near El Alamein, Egypt*

The time was a little before 5:00 A.M. British tanks revved up engines. At precisely 5:00 the Eighth Army would launch what Montgomery called Operation Supercharge—a massive blow to blast Rommel out of Egypt and back into Libya.

An American war correspondent, A. C.

American GIs eating—"chowing down," in GI parlance—after digging into positions during the invasion of French North Africa. They are eating from aluminum mess kits, which consisted of a plate, a cup, and utensils. The Quartermaster Corps tried to truck hot meals to front-line troops like these. When hot food didn't arrive, troops ate "C" rations, canned food that included Spam, a canned meat that could be heated but which most GIs came to detest because they ate it so often. *(Photo courtesy of the National Archives)*

Sedgwick, was riding on a tank toward the German lines. Later he described the scene:

"Tanks moving up in battle make an impressive sight and sound. The mass of engines laboring in low gear can be heard a great distance away. Close by, one cannot be heard when he uses an ordinary conversational tone. . . . One imagines that miles of heavy chain are being drawn over sheets of corrugated iron.

"One seldom sees a tank on the move except as something almost ghostly in an enveloping cloud of dusty yellow. . . . The nose of each snorting, protesting monster protrudes into the cloud of dust created by the tank ahead of it. The exhaust continually emits blue and red fire. . . .

"The guns of the tank make a sharp, metallic ring of flashes that seem to turn the dust cloud into a rosy fire. Occasionally a turret opens and a man looks out. Often he continues to stay in that exposed position despite the fire of enemy guns."

**Nov. 2:** *El Alamein, Egypt, Rommel's headquarters*

A month ago the Desert Fox and his 96,000 Italians and Germans had come here, snapping at the heels of the fleeing Eighth Army. Rommel had begged for more fuel and tanks to crack through the British. Now he had little fuel, few tanks, and 59,000 of his men had been killed, wounded, or captured. He sent a message to Hitler reporting that he would begin the retreat back to Libya with the bloodied remnants of his army—about 25,000 Italians, 10,000 Germans, and 60 battered tanks.

Hitler radioed a reply: "The situation demands that the positions at El Alamein be held to the last man. A retreat is out of the question. Victory or death. Heil Hitler!"

Rommel shrugged. He ordered his battered army to begin the long, hot journey through the desert back to Libya. He knew his wounded and his weary troops would be bombed and strafed each step of the way by a Royal Air Force that had swept the African skies clear of the Luftwaffe.

**Nov. 7:** *Moscow, the Kremlin*

General Georgi Zhukov nervously rubbed a hand across his bald head as he assured Stalin that their plan, code-named Operation Uranus, was now ready for launching. Uranus called for 500,000 troops, 1,000 new tanks, 13,500 new guns, and 1,000 planes to strike north and south of Stalingrad.

"The Germans," said Zhukov, "are being drawn to Stalingrad like the moth to the flame." The bulk of the German army in the Caucasus had plunged into Stalingrad. Its flanks were shielded on the north and south by weak Rumanian armies. Operation Uranus would throw 250,000 fresh Russians at the Rumanians north of Stalingrad, another 250,000 at the Rumanians south of Stalingrad. The north dagger and the south dagger would pierce the Rumanians, then turn and come together behind the Germans, trapping them in battle inside Stalingrad.

Stalin signed a paper, approving Uranus. The attack was set for dawn on November 19.

**NOV. 8:** *2,000 feet over Oran, Algeria, in French North Africa*

The lumbering transport plane, loaded with American paratroopers, roared toward the target area. The pilot could see hundreds of chutes blossoming in the sunlight ahead of him as other transport planes, flying from England, came over the drop zone.

The Messerschmitt 110 flashed down out of the moonlight and streamed bullets at the weaving transport. One bullet tore into Private John Mackall, from Wellsville, Ohio. He became the first American soldier to die in the invasion of North Africa.

**NOV. 8:** *The Atlantic, off Casablanca, French Morocco*

Sergeant John Anspacher ducked low as his assault boat churned through the darkness toward the coast. The search light of French coastal guns had picked out the boat, one of thousands ferrying General Patton's 35,000 Western Force troops ashore. Some 500 to 1,000 miles away, almost 60,000 Americans and

British were landing from the Mediterranean onto beaches at Oran and Algiers in French-owned Algeria, which bordered on Tunisia and Libya.

Anspacher heard the rattle of a machine gun. Bullets spattered around the assault boat. Moments later its steel prow hit the coral-lined shore with a grinding crash. Water poured into the boat.

"Every man overboard!" shouted an officer.

Anspacher plunged into the white surf. Waves washed over his head. His sixty-pound pack, soaked with seawater, pulled him below the huge breakers. Gasping and choking, he reached for a hunk of coral, but the surf pulled him back out to the sea. He heard screams for help.

A soldier's hand grasped his arm and pulled him onto a rock. He scrambled over sharp coral, cutting his hands, and flopped, gasping, in a grove of fruit trees.

He heard a sharp whine, then a second. Explosions lifted his body off the ground. Dirt fountained high into the air around him. French artillery was firing at the Americans as they came ashore.

**Nov. 7:** *Shangri-la, President Roosevelt's retreat in the Maryland hills*

Usually in an affable mood at his secret hideaway, President Roosevelt seemed tense after a late-night dinner with his closest aide, the skinny, rumpled Harry Hopkins.

They knew that the Torch landings were taking place at this very moment.

The phone rang. His secretary, Grace Tully, said the War Department was calling. The President's hand shook as he took the phone. He listened for several moments, then shouted to his caller and to Tully and Hopkins: "Thank God, thank God. That sounds grand. Congratulations. Casualties are comparatively light, much below your predictions. Thank God."

He put down the phone and said almost to himself, "We have landed in North Africa . . . we are striking back."

**NOV. 8:** *Munich, a beer hall*

Speaking at an annual get-together of his Nazi Party faithful, Hitler looked tired, even sickly, his face pale and jowly. But his followers laughed as he jibed at his enemies.

"Now that chief crook, Roosevelt, comes along and says he will save Europe by invading Africa. He would have been better off saving his 13 million unemployed during the Depression. Instead he plunged the world into war."

*"Sieg Heil! Sieg Heil! Seig Heil!"* roared the Nazis.

They roared even louder when he promised them that "a certain city in Russia, you know it well by its name, will soon be ours."

**Nov. 8:** *A beach near Casablanca*

His pearl-handled pistol strapped to his side—he had once killed a Mexican guerrilla fighter with it—Major General George Patton strode up and down the beach. He bellowed at troops to unload boats at a faster pace. A French fighter plane zoomed low and strafed the beach. Soldiers ducked behind boats, but Patton stood erect as bullets kicked sand onto his polished boots. When the plane buzzed off, he told the troops, "We are going to stay on these beaches in Africa whether dead or alive, and if alive we shall not surrender."

His troops began to advance against French fire toward Casablanca. Patton rode in his tank, often at the head of a column. "If you stopped during an advance," a soldier said later, "suddenly he was there coming down on you like the wrath of God."

A bunch of infantrymen stopped as French shells rained down on them. Patton grabbed the unit's commander and snapped, "If your troops don't move forward, don't you come back—except in a box."

**Nov. 9:** *On the Central Front 100 miles from Moscow*
Snow and wind had whipped at his face all day. Now, with numbed fingers, Wilhelm Hoffman of the 267th Regiment of the German Ninety-fourth Division scribbled in his diary. He sat huddled in a farmhouse, the temperature below zero, a blizzard piling twenty-foot drifts across the barren steppes. This would be his second winter in Russia, and Hoffman dreaded facing its icy misery. "Every German soldier," he wrote, "sees himself as a condemned man."

Bob Hope (left) was fighting his own war in *Road to Morocco*, a 1942 film showing in theaters while American GIs were fighting for real in French Morocco. By 1942 Hope had flown twice to overseas battle areas to entertain the troops. (Photo from the author's collection)

**Nov. 11:** *Munich, aboard Hitler's armored train enroute to Wolf's Lair in eastern Germany*

As the train roared out of the city, Hitler reviewed the orders he had issued. His troops were marching into Vichy and the rest of France the Germans had not already occupied. He knew the French in North Africa would quickly lay down their arms and surrender Algeria and French Morocco to Eisenhower's invading armies. Hitler wanted troops in the south of France to guard against an American invasion from their newly won bases in North Africa.

He had decided to take on the Americans in French North Africa. He ordered more than 200,000 Italians and Germans rushed to Tunisia, the French colony sandwiched between Libya and Algeria.

Rommel, he knew, was rumbling toward Libya with his shattered Afrika Korps. Those 200,000 fresh troops would enable Rommel to keep the English and Americans busy for six months while Hitler seized Stalingrad. Then he could turn his full might on the English and Americans trapped in North Africa.

**Nov. 12:** *Kaiser shipyard, Richmond, California*

In World War I, a 10,000-ton cargo ship was built in 200 days. On this day, the Kaiser shipyard turned out a Liberty ship in seven days—a record. "Nuts to seven days," Henry J. Kaiser told his men and women workers. "Let's go for five days."

**Nov. 13:** *A hundred miles off Guadalcanal*

The American warships cut through the inky-black darkness searching for Japanese transports carrying troops to Guadalcanal. As guns flashed, a Japanese submarine commander saw the cruiser *Juneau* outlined in the night sky. He fired a torpedo that hit amidship. A huge ball of white light lit up the Pacific night as the *Juneau* cracked in two, her ammunition blowing up. More than 1,000 officers and sailors were thrown into the dark ocean swells. Other warships rushed by, in the confusion leaving hundreds of the *Juneau* men to drown. Among them were five sailors named Joe, Frank, Al, Madison, and George Sullivan—five brothers.

**Nov. 15:** *Washington*

President Roosevelt read a cable from General Eisenhower, who had set up headquarters in Algiers. General Patton had captured Casablanca and the rest of French Morocco. The armada's two landing forces had taken Oran and Algiers, Algeria's two big Mediterranean ports. Eisenhower was massing troops on the Algerian border to plunge into Tunisia. He reported that the Germans had already flown in 10,000 troops from Europe and thousands more were arriving each day.

Eisenhower's armies had captured all of French Morocco and French Algeria at a cost of 360 dead and 1,050 wounded—"unexpectedly light casualties," Eisenhower reported.

A top Vichy French official, Admiral Jean Darlan, had been captured in North Africa. Darlan had helped the Nazis transport thousands of French workers and Jews to German factories or concentration camps. Darlan told Eisenhower that he could get French generals and admirals to surrender Morocco and Algeria to the Allied invaders. Ike wanted quick victories in Algeria and Morocco so he could capture Tunisia before Hitler massed too large a force. Eisenhower named Darlan governor of French North Africa with Henri Giraud as military commander.

People in America and England shouted angrily that Darlan was one of Hitler's gang, a war criminal who should be imprisoned.

Aides like Henry Morgenthau, the treasury secretary, asked Roosevelt how he could stomach having a Hitlerite on his side. Roosevelt quoted what he called an old Bulgarian proverb, "My children, you are permitted in time of great danger to walk with the Devil until you have crossed the bridge."

**Nov. 17:** *Washington, the Shoreham Hotel*

Speaking to newspaper editors and by radio to the nation, President Roosevelt said that America had fought the Axis tide to a standstill in 1942. The time had now come, he said, to turn back the tide. "It would seem," he said, "that the turning point of this war has finally been reached."

**Nov. 18:** *Washington, the White House*

After signing into law a bill that allowed the drafting of eighteen- and nineteen-year-olds, President Roosevelt said that too many men were switching from low-paying jobs on farms to higher-paying factory jobs. Any man who switched jobs, he said, would be inducted into the Army.

**Nov. 19:** *Serafimovich, a village north of Stalingrad*

The time was just before 6:30 A.M., the dawn breaking on a foggy day with snow beginning to fall. The Rumanian soldiers awoke in their straw-filled trenches to see orange and red flames stab across the skies. Almost 4,000 Russian guns were pouring shells straight at them—the beginning of the Uranus offensive to trap Hitler's armies in Stalingrad.

Soldiers shrieked with fear. Shell bursts "walked" up and down the trenches, each burst pouring tons of dirt onto the men. Hundreds suffocated to death. Some bolted from the trenches to be blown into fragments. Soldiers ran wildly, lost amid funnels of black smoke.

After an hour the cannons stopped. In the sudden hush, the Rumanians saw hundreds of huge Russian tanks rumbling out of the smoke, coming straight at them.

Rumanians turned and ran hysterically into the thickening blizzard.

**Nov. 22:** *Near Kalach Bridge, west of Stalingrad*

The Russian tank commander, Colonel Grigor Fillipov, steered his T-34 tank through the wind-whipped snow. He saw the bridge straight ahead, guarded by German .88 gun crews. Fillipov's four other tanks clanked behind him.

The five Russian tanks roared by the Germans, who thought these were captured Russian tanks being driven by Germans. The German garrison at Kalach had no idea that the jaws of the two Russian armies, attacking from the north and south of Stalingrad, were now aiming to slam shut at Kalach, trapping the German Sixth Army.

A German sergeant grabbed binoculars and peered closely at the five tanks. "Those tanks are Russian!" he shouted. His gun crew fired, and two Russian tanks exploded into balls of fiery orange flame and black smoke.

Colonel Fillipov leaped out of his tank and commanded the other two tanks to direct their shells on the German guns. He ducked behind a hedge and began a radio call for help in holding this bridge.

**Nov. 23:** *Sovetsky, near Kalach Bridge*

The green flares shot high into the air, the signal from the Russian force advancing from the north to the tanks rushing from the south that each was Russian.

The Russian T-34 commander saw German soldiers firing a machine gun at a crossroad leading into Sovetsky. The T-34's cannon roared, and the German gun crews vanished, blown to bits by a shell that could disintegrate an airplane.

Moments later the tank commander saw hundreds of white-clad soldiers running down the road toward him, firing green flares high into the dusk. They were Russian troops from the south meeting the tanks from the north.

The Russian jaws had closed, coming together at Kalach Bridge to form a ring of steel around nearly 300,000 Germans trapped inside Stalingrad.

**Nov. 25:** *Wolf's Lair, Hitler's Russian headquarters in eastern Germany*

The hook-nosed, silver-haired Field Marshal Fritz von Manstein had just arrived by plane from north Russia. Hitler looked upon Manstein as his good luck charm. Manstein had rammed his armies through France in six weeks. He had captured the Russian fortress of Sevastopol in six days.

Manstein told Hitler that he could save the trapped Sixth Army, but it must break out of Stalingrad. Manstein would ram a rescue army at the Russians. The Russians would be caught between the two German armies, which would link up outside Stalingrad.

"No!" shouted Hitler. He demanded that Manstein ram his rescue army through the Russian ring and break into Stalingrad.

Manstein knew a breakthrough was next to impossible. But he shot out his right arm in the Nazi salute, shouted "Heil Hitler!" and went off to organize a rescue army.

**Nov. 30:** *Port Moresby, New Guinea*

Lt. General Bob Eichelberger came up the steps of the bungalow where MacArthur lived. MacArthur had moved from Australia to get closer to the fighting. By now the survivors of General Horii's ill-fated force had arrived at Buna on New Guinea's north coast. They had been reinforced by more than 5,000 troops landed at Buna from the sea. Now 7,500 strong, the Japanese had blasted the American and Australian forces sent to wipe them out. MacArthur could not begin his Pacific offense—an island-by-island hop back to the Philippines—if he did not wipe out the Japanese at Buna, erasing the Japanese threat to invade Australia.

MacArthur told Eichelberger that the Japanese held the higher ground at Buna. They hid in bunkers built with hard logs and perched in trees to pick off the GIs and Diggers slipping and sliding up the muddy trails. Panting in the steamy jungle heat, bitten by insects and giant rats, American soldiers were no match against tough and hardened Japanese bush fighters. Australians angered MacArthur by telling him the GIs at Buna should be replaced by an all-Australian army.

MacArthur told Eichelberger to take over the army at Buna. "If you capture Buna," Mac-Arthur told the stumpy Eichelberger, "I'll award you the Distinguished Service Cross."

Eichelberger saluted and turned to leave. "Bob," MacArthur said grimly, "take Buna or don't come back alive."

## Chapter Twelve

**DEC. 1:** *Aboard the cargo ship* Syros *in the Arctic Ocean bound for Murmansk, Russia*

This was eighteen-year-old Merchant Marine Cadet Ray Holubowicz's first voyage. His cargo ship, part of Convoy PQ-16, plowed through the mountainous waves and whistling winds from the Arctic Circle on the last leg of a run from Boston to Murmansk. The ships carried guns and tanks to Stalin's armies.

Pacing the bridge and wrapped in his pea coat, Ray scanned the skies for German Junkers. Flying from the northern tip of Norway, the Junker bombers had attacked the convoy twice in the past twenty-four hours. From here on, a seventy-three-year-old mate told Ray, the merchant ships and their guardian destroyers would run a gauntlet. The Germans would hammer the ships with torpedoes and bombs from nearby submarine and air bases.

Ray saw the pennant rise swiftly on a destroyer—the signal that subs had been detected. Then he saw the torpedo's white wake arrowing toward the *Syros*.

"Wheel hard over!" he shouted to the helmsman.

The prow of the *Syros* swung away from the incoming torpedo, but it caught the *Syros* near midship. Ray heard the blast as the ship rocked, hurling him against the bridge's railing. Two more explosions shook the bridge.

"It hit the engine room!" he told himself. His best friend, John Brewster, another cadet from Kings Point, worked in the engine room.

The ship was wrapped in a white sheet of flame. Moments later the *Syros* broke in half. Ray slid off the bridge into the Arctic water.

Bobbing up and down, choking and gasping, Ray saw the hulls of the convoy moving away. No cargo ship could stop to pick up survivors. It could be sitting in the cross hairs of a sub's periscope.

A swift Canadian corvette darted through the fog. A lookout saw Ray and other *Syros* survivors. Minutes later, a drenched Ray, shaking with fright and cold, clambered onto the deck of the corvette. He looked at the half-dozen other blanket-wrapped survivors flopped on the deck. His friend John Brewster had gone to the ocean's bottom.

**DEC. 2:** *Guadalcanal*

Huddled in a slimy hole, the marine rifleman had poured fire at a Japanese machine gun for the past hour. As darkness fell over the jungle, the firing ceased. He fell asleep, then awoke, hearing a voice whisper his name.

"Private Holle?"

A sergeant told him to go back to a command post a few hundred yards away.

A marine major met him at the command post and asked, "Are you Private George Holle of Eau Claire, Wisconsin?"

"Yes, sir," lied the tall, lanky Bill Holle.

"We got a cable that your stepfather has died. You've inherited his estate."

The major paused. "This message also says that you're only thirteen years old."

The brawny twelve-year-old Bill Holle had enlisted in the Marines a year ago, using the papers of a relative, George Holle. Bill Holle was told that the nation's youngest fighting man was being sent home. "When I'm seventeen," he said to the major, "I'll join again."

**DEC. 2:** *Chicago, Illinois, Stagg Field*

The University of Chicago's football team had won and lost games at this field. Now, under the rickety wooden stands, atomic-bomb researchers bent over a counter. One scientist, Enrico Fermi, watched the dial as the counter's clickety-clack-clickety-clack became almost a roar.

Fermi raised a hand and said in his soft, Italian-accented voice, "The pile has gone critical."

Other physicists knew what he meant. For the first time, humans had controlled the release of atomic energy. American scientists had taken their first big step toward building an atomic bomb.

Someone brought in a bottle of wine to celebrate the success of years of experiments. As they sipped wine, scientist Leo Szilard said to Fermi, "I think this day will go down as a black day in the history of mankind." No, said Fermi. If an atomic bomb would make war too much of a horror for any future Hitler to contemplate, he told Szilard, this would be a golden day for mankind.

### DEC. 2: *Stalingrad*

"Manstein is coming! Manstein is coming!"

German soldiers shouted the happy news as they ducked between wrecked buildings. Icicles hung from the walls of rooms where the soldiers took shelter from blasts of wind and snow. Manstein had conquered France. He would free them from what they called "this mousetrap."

His face was too frozen for twenty-year-old Private Ekkehert Brunnert to smile at the news. His clothes were iced to his skin. Pains knifed his stomach. His big meal each day was watery soup. And privates got one bowl only.

He lived in a snow-lined hole. Snipers shot at him from rooftops 100 yards away. At night he crawled out of the hole and searched for food. Yesterday he found the head of a frozen horse. Its brains had given him his most filling meal in a week.

### Dec. 5: *Buna, New Guinea*

American war correspondent Murlin Spencer crawled toward the forward trenches of the Americans besieging the Japanese along the shoreline. Two GIs, Private Stanley Orlowski and Sergeant Ron McCann, crouched in a muddy foxhole. Their M-1 Garand rifles pointed at trees no more than a baseball throw away. Spencer saw a corporal nearby lift his head to fire, then heard the mosquito-buzzing sound of a bullet fired by a Japanese rifle. The corporal slumped, blood running from his neck. A corpsman helped him stumble back to an aid station.

An American machine gunner hosed the trees with bullets. Orlowski and McCann pumped rifle shots. "You got one!" a soldier shouted at McCann.

"Darned right I did," McCann said. "He's my eighth."

Darkness settled over the beach and its nearby jungle. Spencer could hear only the pounding of waves. Buna village sat quietly, nothing moving in the moonlight. Then the American artillery began to fire from a mile back. "There was a dull crack as the guns fired," Spencer wrote later. "Then the whine of a shell almost like the whine of a dog. Then finally came a deafening explosion from Buna village."

The Japanese retaliated by rifling grenades at the Americans in their foxholes. "No one dared to move," reported Spencer. When the grenades landed, they shook the ground. Deadly pieces of jagged metal flew over his head, but he wasn't hit. Near dawn he and the other Americans slept fitfully in their holes. At sunup an American rose to relieve himself. Bullets zipped by him. Spencer crawled to the rear.

"All that is life to the American soldier in this jungle," Spencer wrote that afternoon. "They take it day after day. I took it only an afternoon and a night and for me it was nerve-wracking."

**DEC. 6:** *Washington, the White House, the Oval Office*

President Roosevelt named the lanky, balding secretary of agriculture, Claude Wickard, as the "dictator" of the nation's food program. Wickard, he said, would decide what foods would be rationed and how much food each family would be allowed per week. The Army and Navy and other United Nations troops, Roosevelt said, were consuming almost half of the nation's food supply.

**DEC. 14:** *Dubno, Russia*

A German engineer, Hermann Graebe, was building army depots in Ukrainian towns captured by the Germans. Two months ago he had stopped in this village and watched a German Extermination unit round up about 5,000 local Jews. He told an interviewer years later what he had seen:

"Without screaming or weeping, these people undressed, stood around in family groups, kissed each other, said farewells and waited for a sign from [a] S.S. man, who stood near them with a whip in his hand. . . .

"An old woman with snow-white hair was holding a one-year-old child in her arms and singing to it as the child cooed. . . . The father was holding the hand of a boy of about 10 years old and speaking to him softly. The boy was fighting his tears. The father pointed to the sky, stroked his head, and seemed to explain something to him. . . .

"I walked around the mound and found myself confronted by a tremendous grave. People were closely wedged together and lying on top of each other so that only their heads were visible. Nearly all had blood running over their shoulders from their heads. Some of the people were still moving. Some were lifting their arms and turning their heads to show they were still alive. . . .

"I looked for the man who did the shooting. He was an S.S. man who sat at the edge of the narrow end of the pit, his feet dangling into the pit. He had a tommy gun on his knees. . . .

"The people, completely naked, went down some steps and clambered over the heads of the people lying there at the place to which the S.S. man directed them. . . . Then I heard a series of shots. I looked into the pit and saw that the

German soldiers get ready to spring from their trench for an assault on the Russian defenders of Stalingrad. Fear shows in the eyes of the soldier with a pipe clenched in his teeth. He was well aware that this smoke might be his last. Corpses piled up so high each day during the Stalingrad struggle that they could not be counted with accuracy. (Photo courtesy of the National Archives)

bodies were twitching or the heads lying motionless on top of bodies that lay beneath them. . . . The next batch was approaching already. . . . They went down into the pit, lined themselves up against the previous victims, and were shot."

**DEC. 20:** *Verkhne-Kumski, twenty-five miles south of Stalingrad*

German tanks clanged against Russian tanks. Machine guns sprayed bullets wildly, hitting friend and foe. Bodies seeping blood hung from the sides. Black smoke filled the streets.

Russian T-34s had swept into the town to block Manstein's rescue army. A German tank commander radioed that he had to retreat.

A colonel radioed the commander and ranted: "Is this what you call an attack? I am ashamed."

The tank commander ordered one more charge to break through the Russians. An hour later German tanks rumbled north toward Stalingrad, rolling past dozens of wrecked and burning T-34s, their crews scorched corpses.

**DEC. 23:** *Stalingrad, Sixth Army headquarters*

General Paulus sent a radio message to Manstein. Paulus wanted permission from Hitler for Paulus's Sixth Army to break out of Stalingrad and try to link forces with Manstein's rescue army. With two hands they might claw free of the Russian grip.

Hitler still refused to give up Stalingrad. He foamed at the mouth when he uttered the name of that city.

"It would be impossible to break through to Stalingrad," Manstein radioed Hitler, "without added troops which [are] not available."

Manstcin radiocd Paulus and repeated his message to Hitler. "Well, that's the lot. Good luck, Paulus."

**DEC. 23:** *Vassilevska, south of Stalingrad*

The tanks of the Sixth Panzer Division reached a bridge near here. They were the closest unit to Stalingrad. They shot flares into the night sky, hoping the Sixth Army soldiers could see them some fifteen miles away.

As the flares blossomed in the sky, the division's commander got the order from Manstein: Roll back from Stalingrad—the rescue attempt had failed.

Tank crews wept openly in the frigid night air. As the tanks growled southward, officers stood in their turrets, faced north, and threw farewell salutes to doomed comrades waiting for a rescue army that would never come.

**DEC. 24:** *Buna, New Guinea*

A year ago most of these American soldiers had been sipping malteds, studying books, working as clerks or laborers or factory workers, most of them in small midwestern towns. A year ago today, they had decorated trees and bought Christmas presents.

Today they plodded down trails in a foreign jungle as Bob Eichelberger gathered his troops for a final assault on the Japanese massed along the beaches.

An American observer, George Johnston, watched one regiment advance toward a web of Japanese forts that had mowed down waves of American attackers.

"Most of the kids looked terrified," Johnston later wrote. "Many held their heads in their hands. A few were weeping—probably from nervous strain."

**DEC. 24:** *Near Souk-el-Khemis, Tunisia*

General Eisenhower pulled up to corps headquarters in his armored car. He ran through monsoonlike rain and ankle-deep mud to the tent of his corps commander.

German tank attacks had sent the Americans reeling back toward Algeria. As rain dripped down his round face, Eisenhower winced as he was told that the rain and mud had forced the postponing of an American counterattack against the German army in Tunisia. "We can't move trucks or tanks in this mud," the commander told Ike. "And the natives tell us we will get these torrential rains for six to eight weeks."

Ike winced because Churchill and Roosevelt had expected him to take all the North African ports by early January. He had fallen behind schedule. By now he knew that Hitler had filled

Tunisia, a small, finger-shaped, mountainous country, with more than 250,000 crack troops and huge new Tiger tanks.

Ike also knew that Rommel—the legendary Desert Fox—would soon reach Tunisia from Libya to take command of that army. If Rommel could continue to stall Eisenhower, more than 100,000 United Nations troops would be locked up here in Tunisia. Without the ports of Tunis and Bizerte, there would be no springboard to invade Italy or southern Europe in the spring of 1943. And there would not be enough ships and troops for a cross-channel invasion of France in the fall of 1943.

Hitler had grabbed the key to Europe's back door—Tunisia—away from Eisenhower. And Ike would now have to battle the Desert Fox to get it.

That evening Ike sat down to dinner with the corps commander as rain and sleet pounded the canvas tent. A motorcycle messenger came in, dripping rain. He had a message from Algiers for Ike: Admiral Darlan had been murdered.

### DEC. 25: *Algiers, Algeria*

His aides told General Eisenhower that a local French fanatic had shot Darlan. The assassin had been executed, and no one knew for whom he had been working in the murky world of French African politics. Ike named General Giraud to succeed Darlan. Now, said

Ike, he could do what Marshall had just told him to do: Leave politics alone "and give . . . complete attention to the battle in Tunisia."

**DEC. 25:** *A street in Stalingrad*

T he soldier sang a favorite Christmas carol, "*O Tannenbaum, O Tannenbaum, wie treu sind deine Blatter* . . ." The words swelled off the bullet-pocked walls of the garage. The icy wind swirled through cracked windows, numbing bodies of the huddled soldiers, toes and fingers turned black and gangrenous by frostbite.

Captain Gerhard Meunsch parceled out a thimble of rum to each soldier, a slice of bread, a hunk of horsemeat—their Christmas dinner. They knew that Manstein's rescue army had turned back. Soldiers and officers joined in singing "Stille Nacht." But the caroling stopped after the first few words, memories of other Christmases choking voices and bringing tears.

Meunsch trudged through the falling snow to the captured Red October plant. He toasted Christmas with other officers. A captain suddenly jerked out a pistol and shouted, "Let's shoot each other! None of us will ever get out of here!"

"Take it easy," Meunsch said. Then, on this Christmas night, Meunsch and the captain talked of suicide.

### DEC. 27: *Waterloo, Iowa*

W hen Timothy Sullivan, a railway worker, opened the door, he knew why the naval officer was here. He and his wife had not heard from their five sons for almost two months. The five Sullivan brothers had insisted on serving on the same ship, the *Juneau*. "We're looking after each other," they had written in their last letter. "Keep your chin up."

Mother and father listened as the officer told them that a sub had sunk the *Juneau*. Their five sons were dead. Her surviving child, her daughter, was sobbing, but Mrs. Sullivan kept her chin up. She would not cry, not now, she told herself, not in front of the men.

### DEC. 28: *London, 10 Downing Street*

S ix-foot-five and as erect as the Eiffel Tower, General Charles de Gaulle entered the prime minister's study. The mustached de Gaulle had escaped from France to England in 1940 after leading tanks against the German blitzkrieg. He now commanded Free French soldiers who had fought side by side with the British to retake French Syria. Free French soldiers were now fighting as part of the Eighth Army in North Africa.

Churchill faced de Gaulle across a table. He told de Gaulle that Henri Giraud was the new governor of French North Africa.

De Gaulle nodded agreeably. He would be glad to work with General Giraud. "But the general," he said, "is qualified for a military rather than political role." De Gaulle was making clear to Churchill that he expected to rule postwar France.

After de Gaulle left, Churchill sent a cable to Roosevelt: "I strongly favor a meeting between de Gaulle and Giraud as soon as possible."

Roosevelt and Churchill had decided to meet in Casablanca in early January of 1943. They agreed to invite de Gaulle and Giraud. At this meeting the leaders hoped to map global strategy for 1943.

**DEC. 30:** *Buna, New Guinea*

For a week the American observer, George Johnston, had watched the Japanese and Americans locked in hand-to-hand fighting. The battle lines swayed back and forth in the jungles and on the beaches. Today he saw the same regiment he had watched go into battle so fearfully a week earlier. He wrote: "You would never have believed you were looking at the same men. Their faces were iron, their wrists steel. The only expression in every face was a mixture of hatred and determination. They were tough. . . . They attacked bravely and they killed coldly."

**DEC. 31:** *Buna, New Guinea*

Captain Jefferson Cronk rushed with his company to the water's edge. Machine guns and rifles sprayed Japanese soldiers swimming frantically out to sea. Japanese and American corpses littered the shore.

General Eichelberger crossed a bridge and entered Buna. He radioed General MacArthur that Buna was his. "Buna has been cleared of Japs," a MacArthur aide told reporters. "Australia is safe and MacArthur's army is now ready to start on the road back to the Philippines."

### DEC. 31: *Tokyo, Ministry of War*

Prime and War Minister Hideki Tojo said that Japanese ships could no longer get through the American warships to reinforce and feed the starving Japanese troops on Guadalcanal. He ordered the Japanese survivors to flee the island.

### DEC. 31: *Guadalcanal*

Rows of wooden crosses and Stars of David stretched across the green hill above the Pacific. Mess kits had been used to make aluminum plaques that gave the name of the dead marine or soldier. On one mess kit was this inscription: "Cpl. C.H. Miglin, killed in action 8/20, one swell guy. God bless him."

KAI-SHEK

CHURCHILL

EISENHOWER

HITLER

MACARTHUR

MARSHALL

ROMMEL

ROOSEVELT

STALIN

# CHIANG KAI-SHEK

1887–1975

The son of peasants, Chiang Kai-shek (spelled Jiang Jieshi in Chinese) teamed with warlords to form a Nationalist army in the 1920s. He feuded with the Communist leader, Mao Tse-tung (Zedong in Chinese), forced the Communists from the Nationalist Party, and set up a government in Peking (now Beijing). In 1937 a minor clash triggered war between Japan and China. The Japanese cleared Chiang from the major port cities, and he retreated to a mountain hideout in the interior at Chungking.

He and the Communists agreed to come together and force out the Japanese, but both sides often shot at each other. Roosevelt wanted Chiang's armies to tie down Japanese troops in China. Using the Lend-Lease law, Roosevelt sent millions in dollars and weapons as well as two generals. They were Joe "Vinegar Joe" Stilwell, who tried to command Chiang's ground forces, and Claire Chennault, whose Flying Tigers became the aces of China's air force.

Chiang wanted American money but was reluctant to risk his troops in an all-out assault. He claimed that Chennault's airplanes could bring victory. Result: Chennault and Stilwell bickered, and in Stilwell's words late in 1942, "nothing is happening of importance in the CBI [China-Burma-India Theater]."

# WINSTON SPENCER CHURCHILL
1874–1965

Winston Spencer Churchill caught the eyes of Britishers from his earliest years as a bold and dashing soldier, journalist, and author. During World War I he led the British navy as its first lord of the admiralty. During the Great Depression of the 1930s, the English unemployed thought that conservatives like Churchill did not do enough to help them in their plight. But when Allied armies collapsed in early 1940, political chieftains asked him to become prime minister. In 1940 and 1941, his ringing speeches steeled the English will to win. He took control of the army and navy, dictating strategy to generals and admirals, and he schemed to lure America into joining the fight against Hitler.

For the first six months after the attack on Pearl Harbor, he was the dominant one in the Roosevelt-Churchill partnership, winning over the President to his war strategy, much to the anger of American generals.

Military critics still debate whether he was right or wrong in preventing a cross-channel invasion of Europe in 1942.

# Dwight D. Eisenhower

1890–1969

**B**orn in Texas, Eisenhower grew up in Abilene, Kansas, and graduated from West Point in 1915.

His genius lay in organizing people to work as teams. From 1935 to 1939 he helped set up the American-Filipino army under General MacArthur. In 1941 he caught General Marshall's eye with his slick moving of troops in Louisiana maneuvers. Marshall made him chief of war planning and, within eighteen months, the former colonel was wearing three stars as commanding general, ETO.

Eisenhower and Marshall argued strenuously for the invasion of France in 1942, but went along, though unhappily, with the invasion of North Africa. A worrier in private, with dark moods, and often cranky with staff officers, Ike flashed a sunny smile in public that said all was going well. He insisted that his American officers get along well with the British, sending home those who didn't. Churchill began to have doubts about Ike's strategic skills late in 1942 after the Germans beat him to Tunisia. Ike knew that Churchill's confidence in him had dropped, but he also knew that Marshall would back him if the British tried to oust him as ETO commander.

# ADOLF HITLER
1889–1945

Hitler grew up in Linz, Austria. As a teenager, he went to Vienna to attend an art academy, but he was rejected as untalented. Humiliated, he became a homeless person, living in Vienna's slums. When World War I began, in 1914, he joined the German Army, and in the 1920s he joined the new Nazi Party. His fiery anti-Communist, anti-Semitic speeches made him a hero among Germans impoverished by defeat. In 1933 he became Germany's chancellor. When he attacked Poland in 1939, he set off World War II.

Hitler's modern mechanized Panzers and Luftwaffe shattered Allied armies poorly prepared for twentieth-century warfare. He swiftly conquered western Europe, besieged England, and thrust into Russia. His legions swept to Moscow's gates, then were routed by surprise counterattacks. By 1942 his once seemingly invincible army had been bled by millions of casualties, but he forced Axis partners, including Italy, Bulgaria, and Rumania, to pour millions of troops into his attack on Russia. His armies struck at Russian oil fields near Stalingrad and aimed toward an eventual linkup with the Japanese in India. After staggering defeats in Russia and Africa, his generals began plots to kill him.

# DOUGLAS MACARTHUR

1880–1964

MacArthur's father, General Arthur MacArthur, defeated Filipino rebels fighting American ownership of the Philippines in 1901. In 1903 West Point graduate Douglas MacArthur mapped jungle trails in the Philippines. In 1917, as a major on the Army general staff, he convinced congressmen to pass the first draft of Americans into the Army. By the 1930s he was Army chief of staff and fought bitterly with Roosevelt over more money for defense. He retired and became a military adviser to the Filipino army.

In 1941 Roosevelt made him commander of the American-Filipino army. By 1942 he had become the hero that Americans yearned for. They cheered when he escaped from Bataan to Australia declaring, "I shall return!" He railed at Roosevelt and Marshall for not sending him enough troops and weapons, envious that so much was going to Eisenhower in the ETO. But he and Admiral Bill Halsey teamed up with his air general, George Kenney, to build a land, sea, and air amphibious force. "MacArthur's Army"—he made sure that correspondents wrote it that way—was poised as 1943 began to hop from island to island toward the Philippines.

# GEORGE C. MARSHALL

1880–1959

The son of a Uniontown, Pennsylvania, coal executive, George Catlett Marshall attended Virginia Military Institute and went to the Philippines as a young lieutenant. During World War I he rose to become a colonel on the strategy staff of General Pershing, commander of the American Expeditionary Force in France.

He and Douglas MacArthur had run-ins, and MacArthur came away with a lifelong dislike for Marshall. When MacArthur became chief of staff in the 1930s, he refused to promote Marshall. In 1939 Roosevelt asked Marshall to become chief of staff. The silvery-haired Marshall told the commander in chief that he always spoke his mind. Roosevelt just smiled and gave him the job.

Marshall agreed with Churchill and Roosevelt that Germany should be defeated before Japan. But he wanted a 1942 cross-channel invasion of France so that Hitler could not use all his might to crush the Russians. Churchill argued against the 1942 invasion—and won. The "second front" was launched in North Africa, where Marshall thought it of less help to the Russians than a front in France.

# ERWIN ROMMEL

1891–1944

His father an impoverished school-teacher, Erwin Rommel grew up in an army where most generals were wealthy Prussian noblemen. Machines fascinated him, and he became an expert on the strategic use of tanks and armored cars—commanding what the Germans would make famous as Panzer (armored) troops.

The stocky, blue-eyed Rommel caught Hitler's attention in 1940 during the conquest of France. Leading his tanks and armored cars at the front, Rommel used speed and daring to surprise and trap millions of Allied soldiers. He was contemptuous of Hitler's top generals, snapping at General Halder, "What did you ever do in war apart from sit on your backside in an office?"

In 1941 Hitler sent Rommel to North Africa where he organized the Afrika Korps. His tanks advanced, retreated, advanced and retreated again during two years of battling on the deserts of Libya and Egypt. He was probably the only general who disobeyed an order from Hitler not to retreat (at El Alamein) and survived. Instead of firing the field marshal, Hitler handed Rommel his toughest mission: Block the Americans from capturing Tunisia in 1943.

# FRANKLIN DELANO ROOSEVELT

1882–1945

The son of a wealthy New York State merchant, Roosevelt graduated from Harvard and became a lawyer in Manhattan. He ran for Congress in 1912 and soon became one of New York's most popular Democrats. He served in World War I as assistant secretary of the navy, and ran for vice president in 1920. He and his running mate, James Cox, lost. Soon after, he was stricken by infantile paralysis and was bound to a wheelchair the rest of his life. His popularity never waned, however, and in 1932 he was elected president. He would become the first and only president to serve a third term and win a fourth. He steered the country out of the depths of the Great Depression. He despised dictators and sought ways, not always legal, to help England defeat Hitler.

His big grin and reassuring voice heartened Americans during the defeats in 1941. He bowed often to Churchill's ideas for global strategy, infuriating his chief of staff, General Marshall. By 1943 he was less willing to always go along with Churchill. He had a vision of an idyllic and peaceful postwar world not always shared by the more realistic Churchill, who was more distrustful of Stalin's postwar goals.

# JOSEF STALIN
1879–1953

Studying to be an Orthodox priest when he was fifteen, Josef Stalin—"Sosso" to his adoring mother—instead became a revolutionary. To get money for his Communist Bolshevik Party, he planned bank robberies, and was imprisoned eight times by the Czarist government from 1903 to 1917.

After the Communist Bolsheviks overthrew the Czar, Stalin became the right-hand man of the Communist leader, Nikolai Lenin. In Moscow people said, "Lenin trusts Stalin, but Stalin trusts no one." He expanded his power after Lenin's death and executed thousands of Communist leaders during the 1930s.

In 1939 Stalin shocked the world by signing a nonaggression pact with Hitler, who had sworn to destroy Communism. When Hitler attacked Russia in 1941, Stalin demanded help from England and America, including a second front in Europe in 1942. He had begun the war distrusting his generals, but by 1942 he had removed Communist Party commissars from army commands and given complete control to his generals, especially General Georgi Zhukov.

Churchill abhorred the crude, vodka-swilling dictator, but Roosevelt was humored by his peasant ways, calling him "Uncle Joe."

# IMPORTANT DATES

**Jan. 1**   Representatives from twenty-six nations agree to form a United Nations to defeat the Axis powers.   **Jan. 20** At a conference in the Berlin suburb of Wannsee, German officials hear of Hitler's plans for a "final solution" to the "Jewish problem": mass extermination. **Jan. 21**   Rommel's Afrika Korps begin a counter attack against the British Eighth Army.

**Feb. 15**   The British naval base at Singapore surrenders, completing the Japanese conquest of British Malaya.

**March 9**   The Japanese take Java, completing their conquest of much of the Dutch East Indies.   **March 17**   General Douglas MacArthur lands in Australia after escaping from Bataan. He promises: "I shall return!"

**April 3**   The Japanese begin a final drive to push the British, Chinese, and Burmese out of Burma, cutting off China from aid by sea.   **April 9**   About 75,000 American and Filipino troops on Bataan surrender. General Wainwright holds out with 15,000 men and nurses on the island fortress of Corregidor off Manila.

**May 7–8**   In the Battle of the Coral Sea, American warships repulse a Japanese convoy aiming to capture Port Moresby, the base on New Guinea's coast that they need to invade Australia.   **May 6**   Wainwright surrenders Corregidor and its 15,000 troops.

**June 4–7**   In the Battle of Midway, a smaller American naval force fends off a vast Japanese armada sent to capture Midway, the base in the mid-Pacific from which the Japanese planned to invade Hawaii. **June 9**   The Czech village of Lidice is wiped out by Germans avenging the death of Secret Police Chief Reinhard Heydrich. **June 21**   Rommel captures Tobruk and races toward Egypt.

## JULY

**July 21**   Japanese troops land on New Guinea and struggle over mountains toward Port Moresby.

## AUGUST

**Aug. 7**   American marines land on Guadalcanal and other islands in the Solomons captured by the Japanese. **Aug. 30** Rommel attacks the Eighth Army at El Alamein in Egypt, Cairo, and the canal only a few hundred miles away.

## SEPTEMBER

**Sept. 12**   German troops battle the Russians inside Stalingrad, the city Hitler needs to cut off the Russian armies from oil.

## OCTOBER/NOVEMBER

**Oct. 23–Nov. 2**   In the Battle for El Alamein, Rommel cannot break through the Eighth Army. The British begin to chase him back toward Libya. **Nov. 8**   American and British armies land in French North Africa. They capture French Morocco and French Algeria and smash into neighboring French Tunisia. **Nov. 19–23**   The Russians attack near Stalingrad and trap more than 200,000 Germans inside the shattered city. **Nov. 26**   The battle for Tunisia begins. The British and Americans advance from one side as Rommel's Afrika Korps races there from the other side, still chased by the Eighth Army. Hitler sends more than 200,000 troops to help Rommel hold Tunisia. **Nov. 30**   The Japanese army on New Guinea has retreated to Buna, where MacArthur's Australian-American forces begin a battle to wipe them out.

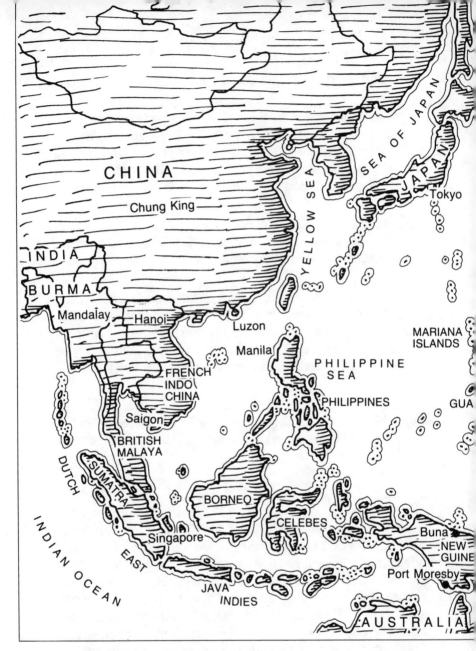

This map shows the war in the Pacific in 1942. The Japanese tried to capture New Guinea as a base to invade Australia. A Japanese invasion fleet was turned back at the Battle of the Coral Sea. The Japanese did land troops at Buna and struck toward Port Moresby. General MacArthur's Australian and American troops harried the Japanese, who got close to Moresby, then fled back to Buna, starving and exhausted by mountainous jungle fighting. MacArthur's troops annihilated the Japanese at Buna, ending Japan's bid for Australia.

ALEUTIAN ISLANDS

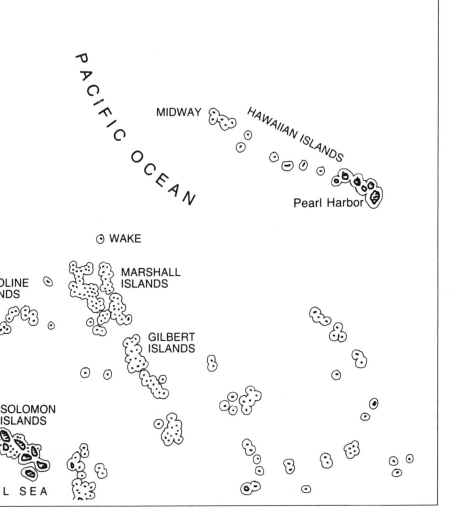

PACIFIC OCEAN

MIDWAY

HAWAIIAN ISLANDS

Pearl Harbor

WAKE

CAROLINE ISLANDS

MARSHALL ISLANDS

GILBERT ISLANDS

SOLOMON ISLANDS

CORAL SEA

American marines landed on Guadalcanal, the first territory recaptured from the Japanese. The Americans turned back a Japanese armada at the Battle of Midway, stopping a Japanese attempt to capture Hawaii. In southeast Asia, the Japanese conquered Malaya, Burma, and the Dutch East Indies. They had cut off supplies coming through Burma to General Chiang Kai-shek's Chinese armies. The Americans and British began plans to recapture Burma.

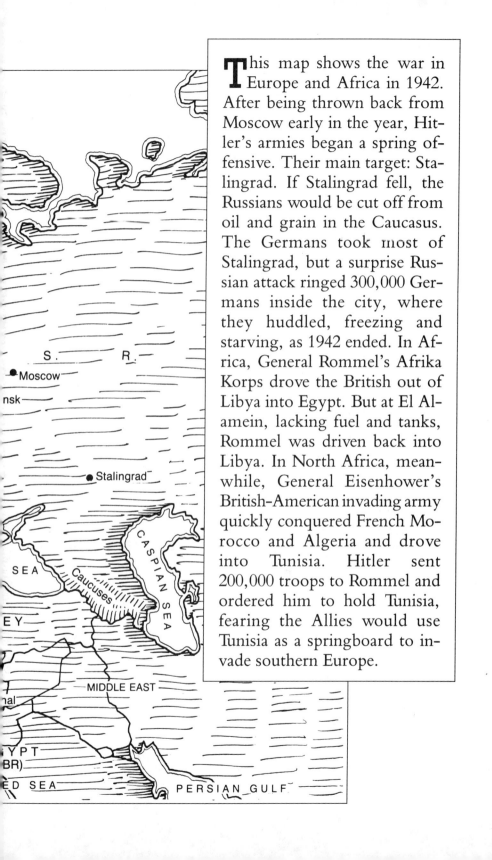

This map shows the war in Europe and Africa in 1942. After being thrown back from Moscow early in the year, Hitler's armies began a spring offensive. Their main target: Stalingrad. If Stalingrad fell, the Russians would be cut off from oil and grain in the Caucasus. The Germans took most of Stalingrad, but a surprise Russian attack ringed 300,000 Germans inside the city, where they huddled, freezing and starving, as 1942 ended. In Africa, General Rommel's Afrika Korps drove the British out of Libya into Egypt. But at El Alamein, lacking fuel and tanks, Rommel was driven back into Libya. In North Africa, meanwhile, General Eisenhower's British-American invading army quickly conquered French Morocco and Algeria and drove into Tunisia. Hitler sent 200,000 troops to Rommel and ordered him to hold Tunisia, fearing the Allies would use Tunisia as a springboard to invade southern Europe.

# FOR FURTHER READING

All the material, including quotations and dialogue, that appears in this book has been taken from newspaper dispatches of 1942, magazine articles and books written during and after World War II. Readers who want to know more about the events that occurred during 1942 can refer to the following list of recommended reading:

Campbell, John. *The Experience of World War II.* New York: Oxford University Press, 1981.

Churchill, Winston. *The Second World War.* Volumes 3 and 4. New York: Houghton Mifflin, 1950.

Craig, William. *Enemy at the Gates, the Battle for Stalingrad.* London: Hodder and Staughton, 1973.

Devaney, John. *Hitler, Mad Dictator of World War II.* New York: Putnam's, 1978.

———. *Douglas MacArthur, Something of a Hero.* New York: Putnam's, 1979.

———. *"Blood and Guts," the Patton Story.* New York: Julian Messner, 1982.

———. *Franklin Delano Roosevelt, President.* New York: Walker, 1987.

Fest, Joachim. *Hitler.* Translated by Richard and Clara Winstin. London: Weidenfeld, 1974.

Long, Gavin. *MacArthur, Military Commander.* London: Batsford, 1969.

Manchester, William. *MacArthur: American Caesar.* New York: McGraw-Hill, 1978.

Morgan, Ted. *F.D.R., a Biography.* New York: Simon and Schuster, 1985.

Mosley, Leonard. *Marshall, Hero for Our Times.* New York: Hearst Books, 1982.

Prange, Gordon W., with Donald Goldstein and Katherine Dillon. *Miracle at Midway.* New York: McGraw-Hill Books, 1982.

Rhodes, Richard. *The Making of the Atomic Bomb.* New York: Simon and Schuster, 1986.

Schultz, Duane. *The Doolittle Raid.* New York: St. Martin's, 1988.

Shirer, William. *The Rise and Fall of the Third Reich.* New York: Simon and Schuster, 1960.

Sommerville, Donald. *World War II Day by Day.* New York: Dorset Press, 1989.

Sullivan, George. *Strange But True Stories of World War II.* New York: Walker, 1991.

Time Editors. *Time Capsule/1942.* New York: Time-Life Books, 1968.

# Index

## 1943: AMERICA TURNS THE TIDE

During the last ninety days of 1942—from October to December—the Axis tide had been stopped at Stalingrad, at El Alamein, on Guadalcanal, and in New Guinea. In the Atlantic the U-boats dived to dodge depth bombs as often as they whistled torpedoes. In skies over Europe, the huge B-17 Flying Fortresses droned toward Germany far more often than Heinkel-111s droned toward England. Even before October, in the Coral Sea and off Midway, the Navy's carriers and battlewagons and torpedo bombers had met the enemy and turned him away from doing what he had done earlier in the year with a swagger.

The United States and its allies fought the Axis tide in 1942 and stopped it. Now at war for a year, by 1943 American men and women were rolling planes, tanks, ships, and guns out of factories and shipyards at a rate never seen before by the industrial world. War workers had a new slogan: "We do the difficult each day. The impossible takes a little longer."

As 1943 began, America poised to turn back the Axis tide and roll it toward Italy, Germany, and Japan. The first stop would be Italy.